A PRIVATE CHEF
SURVIVAL GUIDE

A PRIVATE CHEF SURVIVAL GUIDE

"This essential cookbook is one-of-a-kind!"

CHEF

VOLUME ONE

CHEF KEVIN BENNETT

John 19:30
It is finished, my first cookbook. Hopefully not the last.
Thank you.
Revelations 19:16
Amen.

Chef Kevin

Ecclesiastes 3:22
So I saw that there is nothing better for a person
than to enjoy their work.
Amen.

HIGHLIGHTS

A 400-Item Inventory

A One-Week Menu Outline

Recipes for the One-Week Menu

Prep Time(s) for Each Recipe

Prep Outline/Time for Each Day that Is Achievable

A Private Chef's Survival Guide

TABLE OF CONTENTS

ABOUT THIS BOOK

The goal of this series of cookbooks boils down to this: It is meant to be a practical tool, a go-to guide, a survival guide, a manual. Yes, I think that describes it—a manual for a private chef.

The purpose of creating this new one-of-a-kind cookbook, or call it a success manual for a private chef, is twofold:

First, it will be a cookbook for my past, current, and future guests to enjoy. They will get a cookbook with the recipes that they have eaten so that they can try to make them for themselves.

The second purpose of this cookbook is to give new or existing private chefs a solid foundation to easily prepare and serve meals for a one-week menu.

It might not have fancy pictures of food—maybe someday—and it might not have recipes that a person on the street can follow along with and make. You need to have a foundational sense of cooking to follow and make some of my recipes.

While hopefully more volumes of cookbooks will follow, I just wanted to get volume one published and in the hands of readers. I could have put more things into this book for sure, but I needed to stop somewhere in order to get this one out. Now I'm starting on volume two.

As private chefs we sometimes get complacent and need new information. Hopefully, this book will serve as a refreshing book of new things to do, new recipes, new menus, etc.

As a chef like you, I am constantly buying cooking magazines at the grocery stores and cookbooks that I think will interest me, but I usually only get like one recipe out of them. My book provides so much more:

It's been tested.

It's been used by other chefs. I can tell you that it works.

It's proven.

And I'm giving it to you to use for your own success.

A lot of people inquire, "Is your recipe a secret?" My answer is . . . NO. Let me give it to you because I want you to make it and enjoy it. Food should be great. If I can help you make great food, let me please help you.

My recipes are not written in the traditional step-by-step, paint-by-numbers format. You can take the recipe and follow along with it or spin it off in your own direction and create your version of the dish.

But, if you are a private chef somewhere, such as on a dive boat, charter boat, or yacht, or at a fishing lodge or an estate, this book hopefully will serve as a guide to get you from Point A to Point B.

WHERE IT ALL BEGAN

My *first job at age sixteen* was as a dishwasher at a small hotel restaurant in Greene, New York. Long story short, I then spent about twenty-five years managing restaurants. I did every management position, from senior kitchen manager to general manager, spending about 60 percent of my career as a kitchen manager and about 40 percent as a front-of-house manager. Around 2016, I was between jobs and decided to try to be a personal/private chef.

My first job in the category I consider to be The Private Chef World was with the Aggressor Fleet Dive Boat Company. I signed on with the Big Island Hawaii Boat. It was a one-week charter with fourteen guests and six crew. I was going to name my first cookbook *Cooking for Twenty*, since that is the amount of people I got comfortable cooking for.

I cooked free for all for about one year—no recipes, no rhyme or reason as to what I was doing. Guests started asking me for recipes of what they liked eating, and my reply was, "Sorry, I just cook without recipes." After oh so many requests for recipes of my cooking, I decided to start the process of writing recipes. Let me tell you, it's a time-consuming process, and when you work on a dive boat, time is not on your side. But nevertheless, the recipe/cookbook was born into existence.

Before the idea for this private chef survival guide cookbook evolved, about a year or so into my first private chef job, a staffing situation came up. I was scheduled to go on vacation and we didn't have a relief chef for that time. I had someone on the staff who had some restaurant management background. I spent two weeks training him to do the job, enough so that he could cover for me while I was on vacation.

It was at that point when recipes and clear menus became an important part of the equation.

The thing that sparked my interest was that now someone else was cooking my recipes and I was eating my food cooked by someone else, and I was pleased that I was eating my food that I enjoyed and someone else was able to cook it. The wheels to this cookbook started to turn.

Moving a bit forward, I took a job as a chef at an upscale fishing lodge in King Salmon, Alaska, called Bear Trail Lodge. I also consider this to be in the category of The Private Chef World.

It was there in Alaska where I had the start of a recipe book, and I decided that a private chef would find it useful as a foundation manual. Over four years, my Alaska sous chefs and I mapped out a one-week menu, inventory, and recipes. The last piece to *A Private Chef Survival Guide* would be the timed-out prep daily plan, which makes each day make sense in the world of prep times and the successful cooking of a one-week menu.

The foundation of a one-week menu is just that—a guide. I will call this first week *Volume One* because *Volume Two, Three, Four*, etc. can be an entirely different one-week menu(s). For example, if you serve filet mignon with chimichurri sauce one week, and the next week you serve it with bacon butter, you have essentially offered a different menu item from one week to the next. I also tell people that if you make New England clam chowder one week, change it up—make Manhattan clam chowder the next week. Just an example.

I have concluded that a private chef's job boils down to about 80/20 percent. I think the actual cooking part adds up to about 20 percent of your day/week. Things like doing dishes, taking out trash, cleaning, putting groceries away, shopping, inventory, menu writing/planning, recipe writing, organizing, etc. are all tasks that take up a lot of a chef's time. I've seen a lot of chefs get into this field and fail because of watching too many cooking shows on TV. I think you have to be good at all parts of the job in order for the final product/plates of food to come out consistently great.

I hope this book will serve as a guide for other private chefs and/or lodges, like the ones I worked for in Alaska, to start creating their own cookbook manuals to share with their guests and other private chefs.

Sincerely,

CHEF

INVENTORY

I *offer this 400-item inventory* as a survival guide tool. It has everything and then some to make all of the recipes and menus offered in this cookbook.

Add and delete to it as your private chef jobs take you in different directions.

Normally when a private chef goes to a new job, he or she finds an existing pantry, cooler, and/or freezer with stuff in it. Therefore you would go through everything with your inventory sheets and mark off what you have and then mark what you need to shop for.

It's rare, but I have walked into a new house that has nothing. So it took a couple of days of shopping to get everything.

This inventory has everything needed for all the recipes and menus provided. Ninety-nine percent can be shopped for at a Walmart and a local grocery store. One percent would be found at a specialty store like a local fish market or butcher shop.

Some chefs use the "Stevie Wonder" shopping approach. While it can be done, I suggest using a weekly order guide, menu outline, and consolidated shopping list to do all your grocery shopping. No guessing.

A chef who was about to go into the Private Chef Boat World, a previous coworker of mine, asked me a question.

"What's the most important thing? What's priority one?"

I thought, *What a good question.*

My answer was, "Simple. Your inventory on hand for what you are about to cook for a day, week, whatever, is number one." Your core inventory, provided in this cookbook, should be readily available for your upcoming week.

When you are missing ingredients for recipes, you have to substitute, or go without, that ingredient. And then with some exceptions, your end-game product is not going to be as good. It will happen from time to time, but the less it happens, the better for the guest and the chef's reputation.

INVENTORY LIST

1. Paprika
2. Smoked paprika
3. Kosher salt, Redbox Diamond Crystal only
4. Table salt
5. Black pepper, medium grind only
6. Granulated garlic
7. Nutmeg
8. Cinnamon
9. Cinnamon sticks
10. Cayenne
11. Parsley
12. Tarragon
13. Cumin
14. Chili powder
15. Oregano
16. Dill
17. Cajun seasoning
18. Red pepper flakes
19. Montreal steak seasoning
20. Thyme
21. Rosemary
22. Cream of tartar
23. Garlic salt
24. White pepper
25. Allspice
26. Ground cloves
27. Whole cloves
28. Onion powder
29. Saffron
30. Taco seasoning packets
31. Curry powder
32. Basil
33. Old Bay seasoning
34. Fennel whole seeds

35. Celery salt
36. Sage
37. Star anise, whole
38. Bay leaves
39. Coriander
40. Himalayan pink salt
41. Brown gravy powder
42. Poultry gravy powder
43. Turkey gravy packets
44. Italian seasoning
45. Pickling spice
46. Coleman's dry mustard
47. Maldon sea salt flakes
48. Blackened/ing seasoning
49. Turmeric
50. Dry chives/cilantro dry
51. Hershey's chocolate syrup
52. Caramel syrup
53. Worcestershire sauce
54. A.1. steak sauce
55. Vanilla extract
56. Coconut extract
57. Maple syrup
58. BBQ sauce, variety
59. Coconut milk
60. Applesauce
61. Mae Ploy
62. Marinara sauce
63. Balsamic vinegar
64. Salad dressings, assorted
65. Balsamic vinegar glaze
66. Apple cider vinegar
67. Cocktail sauce
68. Horseradish, jar/fresh
69. Chipotle, cans/sauce only
70. Frank's RedHot
71. Cream of mushroom soup, condensed
72. Tarter sauce
73. Hellman's/Best Food squeeze BTL Mayo—for condiments
74. Teriyaki sauce
75. Artichoke hearts
76. Mataeo salsa
77. Red salsa, variety
78. Salsa verde
79. Cannellini beans, can
80. Sauerkraut, can/fresh
81. PAM pan spray
82. Canola oil/fryer oil
83. Olive oil
84. Extra virgin olive oil
85. Jelly, variety
86. Peanut butter
87. Sambal oelek
88. Yellow mustard
89. Dijon mustard
90. Whole grain mustard
91. Hellman's/Best Food mayo, 1 qt bottle
92. Soy sauce
93. Box whole milk—for backup

94. Box Chardonnay wine
95. Box red wine
96. Sweetened condensed milk
97. Hot sauce, variety
    Tabasco siracha, etc.
98. Salsa variety
    Mateo, mild, medium
    Salsa verde
99. Red wine vinegar
100. White wine vinegar
101. Lemon juice, bottle
102. Lime juice, bottle
103. Liquid smoke
104. Heinz ketchup
105. Fish sauce
106. Tahini
107. Sesame oil
108. Truffle oil
109. Honey
110. Jamaican jerk seasoning, bottle
111. Nacho cheese sauce, bottle
112. Chili beans, variety
    Red beans garbanzo
    Black beans
113. Conch, cans
114. Bake powder
115. Baking soda
116. All-purpose flour
117. Bread flour
118. Sugar
119. Brown sugar
120. Powdered sugar
121. Heath bar crunch/ crumbles
122. Panko breadcrumbs
123. Italian breadcrumbs
124. Coconut flakes
125. Oreo cookie crumbles
126. Bisquick
127. Old-fashioned oatmeal
128. Cocoa powder
129. Ghirardelli brownie, box
130. Chicken base, paste form
131. Tomato base
132. Beef base
133. Clam base
134. Tempura batter box
135. Cornstarch
136. Yeast
137. Country Time lemonade
138. Cold brew iced tea bags
139. Vanilla coffee creamer, individual
140. Half-and-half coffee creamer, individual
141. Instant coffee expresso/ coffee pods
142. Canned green beans
143. Canned chili beans mixture
144. Banana peppers
145. Couscous/Israel
146. Elbow pasta

147. Spaghetti
148. Linguini
149. Angel hair pasta
150. Sundried tomatoes
151. Dill relish
152. Sweet relish
153. Popcorn, microwave
154. Artichoke hearts
155. SPAM
156. Bush's baked beans
157. Sliced almonds
158. Lasagna noodles, no bake
159. Refried beans
160. Tuna cans/Fancy
161. Marshmallows
162. Anchovies/Fancy
163. Maraschino cherries
164. Jumbo pasta shells
165. Raisins
166. Jasmine rice
167. Capers
168. Black beans, can
169. Chickpeas can/garbanzo
170. Roasted red peppers, jar
171. Chopped garlic in oil
172. Graham cracker pie shells
173. Dried apricots
174. Dry cherries
175. Risotto—plain/kits
176. Homestyle Caesar croutons
177. Bacon bits
178. Clams, large 46 oz can
179. Crackers, variety
180. Tortilla chips, variety
181. Splenda/sugar packets
    Sweet'N Low/Equal
182. Vanilla pudding packs
183. Chocolate pudding packs
184. Mandarin oranges, can
185. White chocolate chips
186. Chocolate chips, semisweet
187. Instant grits/polenta
188. Hominy, cans—soup/grits
189. Black olives, sliced
190. Kalamata olives
191. Mixed nuts, salted
192. Cashews, salted
193. Walnuts
194. Macadamia nuts
195. Pistachios
196. Split peas, dry
197. Kidney beans/chili beans
198. Quinoa
199. Green olives, variety
200. Corn, cans
201. Sushi wraps
202. Tomato paste, small cans
203. Diced tomatoes
204. Crushed tomatoes, can
205. Burrito wrap, 12"–13"
206. Taco shells, variety
207. Brown rice, short grain

208. Uncle Ben's wild rice, original recipe
209. Beer batter, box
210. Saltine crackers
211. Dry chickpeas
212. Pickled ginger
213. Marinara sauce, Rao's
214. Alfredo sauce, jar
215. Kahlua
216. Frozen crabmeat, can, 1 lb
217. Black cod/sablefish
218. Rack of veal or ribeye
219. Rack of lamb or chops
220. Salmon
221. Halibut, fresh is best
222. Sliced roast beef
223. Sliced turkey
224. Sliced pastrami
225. Sliced corned beef
226. Prime rib
227. Breakfast sausage, variety
228. Bacon, thick and thin
229. Sliced ham
230. Sliced salami
231. Sliced pepperoni
232. Shrimp, 16/20's or 21/25's
233. Jumbo shrimp, 2–4 ct
234. Chorizo sausage
235. King crab legs/snow crab
236. Ahi tuna sashimi, fresh
237. Baby back ribs
238. Chicken thighs
239. Chicken breast
240. Beef tenderloin
241. Pork tenderloin
242. Cornish game hens
243. Pork belly
244. Chicken wings
245. Hamburger, 93% lean
246. Hamburger, wagyu
247. Mussels, green/black
248. Scallops, size U 10's
249. Calamari, breaded
250. Beef short rib, English
251. Duck breast, maple
252. Duck legs
253. Hot dogs
254. Angus beef hamburger patties
255. Sausage patties
256. Jimmy Dean regular cog
257. Pancetta
258. Andouille sausage
259. Smoked ham hocks
260. Lobster tails
261. Salmon roe
262. Lobster meat, claw
263. Beef ribs
264. English muffins
265. Bagels
266. White bread, sliced
267. Wheat bread, sliced
268. French bread, Texas Toast

269. Baguette bread
270. Ciabatta rolls
271. Croissants
272. Hot dog buns
273. Lobster rolls/sub buns
274. Brioche burger buns
275. Pretzel rolls
276. Hawaiian rolls
277. Kaiser rolls
278. Pizza dough, raw
279. Whole milk
280. Grated Parmesan cheese
281. Shredded Parmesan cheese
282. Individual yogurts
283. Greek yogurt, plain
284. Mozzarella cheese, shredded
285. Jack cheddar cheese, shredded
286. Mexi cheese, shredded
287. Whole eggs
288. Liquid eggs
289. Heavy cream
290. Half-and-half cream
291. Butter, salted
292. Cheddar cheese, sliced
293. Feta cheese
294. Goat cheese
295. Cream cheese
296. Cream cheese, individual
297. Butter, individual
298. Sour cream
299. Coffee creamer, individual
300. Ice cream, vanilla
301. Ice cream flavor, variety
302. Sorbet, vegan
303. Cheesecake, New York style
304. Provolone, sliced
305. Fresh mozzarella, variety
306. Blue cheese, crumbled
307. Cheddar cheese, shredded
308. Swiss cheese, sliced
309. American cheese, slices
310. Ricotta cheese
311. Canned whipped cream
312. Pepperjack cheese, slices
313. Bri cheese, wheels
314. Fontina cheese, blocks
315. Vanilla creamers, individual
316. Mascarpone cheese
317. Ladyfingers
318. Almond milk
319. Smoked salmon options
320. Frozen potato patties/tater tots
321. Orange juice
322. Cranberry juice
323. Pickled ginger
324. Burrito wraps, 10"–13"
325. Cantaloupe
326. Oranges
327. Lemons

328. Limes
329. Bananas
330. Grapes
331. Pears
332. Watermelon
333. Green beans
334. Spaghetti squash
335. Sugar snap peas
336. Ginger
337. Mint fresh
338. Shallots
339. Chives
340. Whole garlic
341. Garlic cloves, cleaned
342. Carrots with stems, variety
343. Bok choy
344. Color cauliflower
345. Raspberries
346. Blackberries
347. Baby rainbow potatoes
348. Sweet onions
349. Eggplant
350. Butternut squash
351. Yukon Gold potatoes
352. Green beans
353. Fresh dill
354. Fresh herbs variety
355. Red potatoes
356. Russet potatoes
357. Fingerling potatoes
358. Yellow onions
359. Red onions
360. Orange carrots
361. Color carrots
362. Cucumber
363. Zucchini
364. Yellow squash
365. Green cabbage
366. Red cabbage
367. Cauliflower
368. Asparagus
369. Green onions
370. Tomato, 5/4 size
371. Grape tomato, variety
372. Color bell peppers
373. Red bell peppers
374. Portobello mushrooms
375. Cremini mushrooms
376. Mushrooms, variety
377. Broccoli
378. Celery
379. Honey Crisp apples
380. Avocados
381. Romaine hearts
382. Iceberg lettuce
383. Baby spinach
384. Frozen spinach
385. Frozen creamed spinach
386. Spring mix lettuce, variety
387. Arugula
388. Jalapenos
389. Fennel
390. Broccolini
391. Cilantro, fresh

392. American curly parsley
393. Basil fresh
394. Italian flatleaf parsley
395. Pineapple
396. Strawberries
397. Blueberries
398. Honeydew melon
399. Kiwis
400. Radish variety/beets

ONE-WEEK MENU

A*gain, this first* **Volume One** *cookbook* is being put out for private chefs to have a starting point to reference.

As a private chef, use this cookbook as a tool, and go in different directions of your own as time allows. One habit I will suggest is that in some way start compiling your own cookbook. It can be some of your recipes or recipes you find that you like from Google or a magazine, etc. Only keep time-tested recipes that you and your guests like. No need to keep a so-so recipe on hand.

BREAKFAST

Welcome to waking up at 4:30 a.m. Ha ha! Welcome to Private Chef World, where you start your day at around 5:00 a.m. and finish at about 8:00 p.m. or so. Yes, please don't do the math—it's a lot!

I have found that the after-lunch naptime—whether it's a half hour or an hour or two—is almost essential to surviving the private chef schedule. My suggestion is to schedule it and discipline yourself to do it, even if it's just getting off your feet for a half hour. It helps!

It's best to do your breakfast prep the day before. Anything that can be made into a turnkey prepped item, do it the day before so that you don't have to do it in the morning.

All you should be doing in the morning is turning on the equipment and cooking the product and getting it to the guest. If you discover that you are prepping something during breakfast, then make a note to add it to the previous day's prep.

Below is the foundation of a breakfast menu outline that I have used. It's not meant to all be served at one breakfast, but as a list to pick and choose from to offer a variety of items each day of a one-week menu. Offer what you have the time budgeted to do, and tailor it to your guests' needs.

BREAKFAST

Omelets, variety
Pancakes
Waffles
54   Eggs Benedict
Breakfast burrito, variety
Huevos ranchos
Steak and eggs
Frittata

Egg McMuffin, variety

Scrambled eggs

Eggs to order

French toast

Bacon

Sausage, variety

Yogurt, variety

Fruit bowl

Ham

Maple syrup

Ketchup

Coffee, milk

Cream cheese, butter

Peanut butter, jelly

Orange juice

Cranberry juice

Cereal, variety

Bagels, white bread, wheat bread

English muffins

Fruit smoothie

Potatoes, variety/patties

Tater tots/home fry cubes

~~~

LUNCH

In cookbook *Volume One* I will give you an outline for a one-week menu for lunches. Same rules apply: Start with it and then take it in new directions.

Some private chef jobs will require you to make lunch for a venture away from home base. For instance, at Bear Trail Lodge in Alaska lunch involved eating out on the river while fishing. So, we made the lunch the day before, similar to breakfast.

Again, prep what you can the day before and stay on that schedule. It's the same amount of prep if you do it the day before or if you do it last minute. There are many exceptions to this rule, but if done correctly and planned correctly, the system will work.

Consistently, every day, stay one day ahead on prep.

～～

LUNCH

1	**MONDAY**	Meatballs
58	*Italian*	Stuffed shells
32	**TUESDAY**	Cheeseburger
17	*American*	Ahi tuna wraps
	WEDNESDAY	Fresh fish bake
61	*Mediterranean*	Lamb with Tzatziki
41	**THURSDAY**	BBQ ribs
	American BBQ	BBQ chicken
	FRIDAY	Fried rice
	Asian	Stir-fry

| **SATURDAY** | Jamaican/etc. |
| *Pick a theme* | Southern/etc. |

| **SUNDAY** | Taco buffet |
| *Mexican* | |

Note: Add or subtract any of your favorite lunch themes or culture foods, etc.

LUNCH   *Soups*

122	Ribolitta
126	Italian wedding soup
63	Chili
18	Posole
	Vegetable
108	Clam chowder
80	Smoked salmon chowder
103	Manhattan clam chowder
107	Conch chowder
36	Cream of mushroom

LUNCH   *Sides*

11	Guacamole
	Home fries
	Grilled vegetables
	Fried rice
	White rice/jasmine
	Cucumber tomato dill salad
	Couscous salad
	Pineapple baked beans

12   Mac salad
60   Potato salad
      Salt potatoes
      Quinoa salad
50   Mac and cheese
      Garden salad, variety
      Roasted potato halves

LUNCH/DINNER   SALADS

      Caesar salad
13   Greek salad
      Blue cheese wedge salad
      Garden salad, variety
      Fresh mozzarella caprese salad
94   Watermelon Feta salad
30   Waldorf salad
35   Asian salad

LUNCH/DINNER   HOMEMADE BREADS

29   Focaccia bread
55   Jen's homemade white bread
128   Dutch oven basic white bread

LUNCH/DINNER

DESSERTS

8	Apple crisp
8	Blueberry crisp
89	Tiramisu
24	Crème brûlée
15	Banana bread split sundae
124	Blueberry pound cake
	Cheesecake
	Cheesecake ice cream sundae
22	Cookie pie
95	Eaton mess
120	German chocolate cake
21	Key lime pie
26	Coconut crème pie
132	Bread pudding
104	Pudding layer dessert

APPETIZERS

	Smoked cheeseburger slider
99	Pork belly slider
1	Meatball appetizer
23	Ahi poke with tortilla chips
39	Ceviche
11	Guacamole
6	Hummus
38	Seafood fritters
	Calamari quesadillas
51	Crab cakes

SAUCES

DINNER SIDES

STARCHES

9	Coconut rice
27	Gratin potatoes
33	Hominy grits
40	Kevin's white bean stuffing
44	Brown rice with mango
50	Kevin's mac and cheese
58	Stuffed pasta shells
73	Stuffed bell peppers
127	Oyster stuffing
	Pasta—any kind
	Rice—any kind
	Fried rice
	Roast red potatoes
	Mashed potatoes
	Baked potatoes
	Salt potatoes/smashed

VEGETABLES

	Pineapple baked beans
109	Green bean casserole
106	Cajun carrots
	Creamed spinach
85	Sautéed spinach
77	Coleslaw
	Asparagus
	Broccoli crowns
	Broccolini

Mashed cauliflower
Sautéed mushrooms
Mixed sautéed vegetables
Grilled vegetables
Bok choy sautéed

DINNER

One-Week Menu: Protein Category

	MONDAY	Duck breast
41	TUESDAY	Baby back ribs
37	WEDNESDAY	Halibut Olympia
101	THURSDAY	Filet mignon
	FRIDAY	Crab legs
105	SATURDAY	Prime rib
14	SUNDAY	Salmon

DINNER

One-Week Menu: Protein Category

16	MONDAY	Chicken Scallopini
	TUESDAY	Pork tenderloin
16	WEDNESDAY	Black cod
	THURSDAY	Beef Wellington
	FRIDAY	Lobster tails
3	SATURDAY	Ribeye steaks
118	SUNDAY	Ahi tuna steaks

DINNER
One-Week Menu: Protein Category

	MONDAY	Cornish game hens
	TUESDAY	Stuffed pork chops
	WEDNESDAY	Chilean sea bass
137	THURSDAY	Short ribs, beef
	FRIDAY	Lobster ravioli
	SATURDAY	Rack of veal
	SUNDAY	Fresh fish variety

ALASKA MENUS

One of the key factors in hiring a private chef for a dive boat, charter boat, cruise ship chef job, estate chef job, etc., is a person's ability to be able to handle the workday, workweek, work month, etc. This means a seven-day work week for seven weeks or seven months in a row, 5 a.m. to 9 p.m.

It doesn't matter your chef skills. If you can't do the hours, you won't make it in the long run.

The summary of the Alaska menu format is as follows.

DAILY PREP

One person should be able to complete daily prep in about ten hours or less per day, all while helping with either breakfast service or dinner service or both depending on staff levels and schedule needs.

Daily prep starts at the completion of breakfast clean-up shop and finishes at or before dinner plating needs begin. Daily prep involves prepping the breakfast and lunch items the day ahead of time, or in other words, daily prep is prepping for the next day.

The daily prep person also oversees the lunch buffet setup and breakdown.

Two items are placed on both daily prep and the dinner prep person's agenda:

- Cheeseboard
- Daily fresh bread

Both tasks can be done by either person.

Daily prep is more mechanical and robotic than the dinner prep. Not to use a negative word, but daily prep is best for the least trained person on the team, if there is one.

Dinner prep is designed to be done by one person, including about six hours of prep per day after breakfast. About three hours can be done from 8 a.m. to 11 a.m., and the remaining after break/lunch from 2 p.m. to 5 p.m. At 5 p.m. the dinner prep person needs to start the appetizer/dinner cooking process.

In summary, two chefs can handle the workload of daily prep and dinner prep. However, to avoid a seven-day, fourteen-hours-per-day workweek, a third chef is needed to be able to offer a day-off rotation, as well as what I call a shorter-day rotation.

For example, a shorter day would be either 5 a.m. to 5 p.m. or 8 a.m. to 8:30 p.m.

Working the private chef schedule usually requires a designated break period. I usually take a one- to two-hour break after the completion of the lunch service.

This allows the batteries to recharge going into the dinner service hours.

ALASKA

Daily Prep with Prep Times (minutes)

	Breakfast sandwich	15
	Breakfast sandwich meat	10
	Pancake/waffle	15
	Breakfast meat	15
	Breakfast potato	15
	Breakfast special	20
54	Eggs Benedict	20
	Fruit bowl	15
	Daily sandwich	90
67	Cheese board/popcorn	20
55	Daily fresh bread	30
5	Cookies homemade	60
	Cinnamon rolls/croissants	30
	Employee chicken option	20
	Soup prep homemade	60
	Next day's (days') protein pull	20
	Lunch setup buffet	20
	Fruit water change	15
	Fruit bowl restock	15
	Lodge lunch	30
	New guest side salad	30

Total daily prep: about 10 hours

ALASKA

Monday

		Cheeseboard	20
	App 1	Fajita skewer	40
	App 2	Artichoke dip	45
19	App 3	Smoked salmon platter	25
55		Daily fresh bread	30
	Salad	Caesar	60
	Dressing	Caesar	5
41	Protein	Baby back ribs	40
78	Sauce	BBQ sauce	30
	Starch	Mashed potato bag	5
77	Vegetable	Coleslaw	60
	Dessert	Cheesecake	15

Total prep: 6.25 hours

Today's prep time shortcuts are:
Premade/store-bought Caesar salad dressing
Store-bought mashed potatoes
Store-bought cheesecake

ALASKA

Tuesday

		Cheeseboard	20
31	App 1	Buffalo chicken dip	30
69	App 2	Scallops Mornay	40
	App 3	Quesadillas	30
128		Daily bread	30
	Salad	Greek	60
13	Dressing	Greek	20
	Protein	Duck breast	20
7	Sauce	Chutney	25
	Starch	Wild rice	5
106	Vegetable	Cajun carrots	30
24	Dessert	Crème brûlée	35

Total prep: 5.75 hours

Today's prep time has a better balance.
Shortcut prep item today is only one: the wild rice from a box—
Uncle Ben's.

ALASKA

Wednesday

		Cheeseboard	20
20	App 1	Smoked salmon dip	40
99	App 2	Pork belly sliders	40
38	App 3	Seafood fritters	30
		Daily fresh bread	30
	Salad	Asian	60
70	Dressing	Asian ginger	20
37	Protein	Halibut	50
37	Sauce	Olympia	10
44	Starch	Brown rice	15
	Vegetable	Broccolini	20
22	Dessert	Cookie pie	30

Total prep: 6.08 hours

All categories are made from scratch.
No shortcuts today.

ALASKA

Thursday

		Cheeseboard	20
	App 1	Shrimp cocktail	30
10	App 2	Olive tapenade	15
1	App 3	Meatballs + sauce	40
29		Daily fresh bread	30
	Salad	Blue cheese wedge	60
	Dressing	Blue cheese	5
101	Protein	Filet mignon	45
3	Sauce	Chimichurri	30
27	Starch	Gratin potatoes	70
	Vegetable	Asparagus	30
	Dessert	Ice cream sundae	30

Total prep: 6.75 hours

The blue cheese dressing was store-bought.

ALASKA

Friday

		Cheeseboard	20
	App 1	Mozzarella-stuffed pretzels	30
74	App 2	Sushi rolls	80
	App 3	Reuben sliders	25
		Daily fresh bread	30
	Salad	Garden vegetables, variety	60
	Dressing	Italian	5
	Protein	Crab legs	40
	Sauce	Butter/lemons	20
50	Starch	Mac and cheese	50
	Vegetable	Broccoli sphere	20
21	Dessert	Key lime pie	20

Total prep: 6.67 hours

The salad dressing was store-bought.

ALASKA

Saturday

		Cheeseboard	20
81	App 1	Deviled eggs	45
119	App 2	Seafood cakes	40
41	App 3	BBQ ribs	15
55		Daily fresh bread	30
	Salad	Tomato basil mozzarella	60
	Dressing	Balsamic	10
105	Protein	Prime rib	30
2	Sauce	Béarnaise	30
	Starch	Salt potatoes	20
	Vegetable	Zucchini/yellow squash	20
8	Dessert	Apple crisp	30

Total prep: 5.83 hours

The shortcut prep item today again was the store-bought salad dressing.

ALASKA

Sunday

		Cheeseboard	20
	App 1	Fried cheese sticks	5
75	App 2	Chicken wings	15
23	App 3	Ahi poke	30
		Daily fresh bread	30
30	Salad	Waldorf	60
30	Dressing	Waldorf	15
	Protein	Salmon	60
14	Sauce	Roasted red pepper	30
9	Starch	Coconut rice	30
	Vegetable	Mix veggie sauté	30
	Dessert	Lava cake	5

Total prep: 5.5 hours

The cheese sticks were store-bought.
The lava cake was store-bought.

CHEF NOTES

I *consider the private chef job* to be the top one percent of the jobs in the chef world. You can be out of bed at 4:30 a.m. and finish your day at 9:00 p.m., seven days a week for months at a time job.

Not many people can handle the amount of hours per day/per week. I think this is probably the first make-or-break-you category.

If you want to become a private chef, I would recommend taking a test job on a charter boat where you are the only chef and you do all the work for the one-week charter. You will know quickly if you can or cannot survive the demands of cooking for twenty people for one week with six hours to get all the groceries for the week.

I suggest this method because I don't see the point of spending the time and money to go to chef school if this job is not for you. Let me put it another way—I could go to mechanic school for years, but I don't believe I would ever be a great car mechanic. It's not me. It would be a waste of my time.

My goal as a private chef, wherever or whomever I'm cooking for, or whatever I am cooking, is this: I want people to walk away from the table saying, "This was the best (blank) I ever had."

I try for that with everything I make.

The best steak . . .

The best BLT sandwich . . .

The best mashed potato . . .

The best crème brûlée

Etc.

To conclude, I think to be a successful private chef, it can't be a "job." If it's a job to you, a watch-the-clock type situation, and not a hobby or passion that pays the bills, then find another career.

My father had a job; I have a career.

Or, again, a hobby that I enjoy that pays the bills.

A cruise ship captain whom I worked for said it well. He said that he made the decision to marry his job and gave up the life of having a wife, kids, family, etc. It's one way to look at it.

I hope that this cookbook/workbook will help new and existing private chefs get through their workweek a little better. I hope the book at least gives you a mapped-out foundation that helps you grow in your own direction.

〰

SALT

Salt, salt, salt.

I recommend that you develop and stick to *one* type and brand of salt for your all-purpose go-to salt.

I use Diamond Crystal Kosher Salt (Red Box) (three pounds). I now order it on Amazon because most grocery stores do not carry this product. I find that it is a very light, forgiving salt. Not overpowering.

Salts have many ranges of salt flavor, from mild to very strong. Find a salt you like, make sure you have access to it so you always have it on hand, and *don't change it*.

Salt is your most important, most used seasoning.

GARLIC

I love garlic. I love whole garlic bulbs.

However, for all recipes in this recipe book, I use chopped garlic in oil, or in water. I prefer in oil—store-bought in a jar, not homemade.

Some of my recent recipes, in the 100-plus numbers, call for fresh garlic. I will eventually migrate to using fresh garlic in my recipes.

But, to say it again, original recipes, 100 or below, mostly use chopped garlic in oil, like it or not. Two reasons for this. Being a new private chef, time was not on my side, so buying garlic chopped in oil was one less prep item I had to do.

As a private chef, we should be able to Google and make anything from scratch—but we have to pick and choose what we have time to do on a daily basis and go from there. For instance, one day make your own homemade salad dressing, but the next day use a preferred store-bought salad dressing and spend your time making something else homemade.

They other reason I don't use anything but chopped store-bought garlic in oil is because it is way less potent in flavor than fresh garlic.

Again, I would prefer to use fresh garlic, but for recipe consistency, stick with store-bought for now.

It's on my to-do list to make a conversion factor or make your own, such as one tablespoon chopped garlic yields the same flavor profile as . . . maybe one-half clove of fresh garlic—I'm not sure yet.

DIGITAL THERMOMETER

A digital thermometer is a must-have for any chef. I like the yellow Cooper digital thermometer, which is about twenty to thirty dollars. I order mine on Amazon.

Always have one in your chef jacket, and always have a new backup on hand. How else would you know how or when to pull your Traeger prime rib when the center temp hits 127 degrees?

I can think of no other more important chef kitchen tool than your digital thermometer. Digital is instant read. The old dial thermometers are slow, and it's hard to get a precise reading with them

CHEF KNIFE

The second most important chef tool would be your chef knife. I like the Mercer Genesis eight-inch chef knife. It's heavy-duty and cost-effective—about forty dollars—and lasts me about six months. I order them on Amazon.

TRAEGER GRILLS

A few years ago in Alaska I was introduced to the Traeger smoker grill. I was afraid of it. I don't like change. But my sous chef asked me if he could use it. I said sure. I liked the pork loin he cooked. So, I gave it a try and got hooked.

So far, the Traeger dial temperature-controlled smoker grill has produced excellent, consistent filet mignon, prime rib, pork tenderloin, duck breast, and smoked salmon. I highly recommend that you invest in one. It's worth it, believe me.

SOUS VIDE

Like the Traeger, the sous vide machine was recently new to me, but it is starting to become a menu item favorite. It's a time/temp experiment process, but I've never made better short ribs, chicken, or brisket than I have by using this machine. Anova is a good brand and only about $120. I bought mine on Amazon.

OLIVE OIL/FAT

My professor in college proposed a question to the class: What is the most craved category of food?

No, it's not sugar.

Nope, it's not chocolate.

It's fat.

When you eat a bag of potato chips, what's in your mouth? It's all the oil that saturates the potato.

Salad dressing = fat

Olive oil = fat

Butter = fat

Heavy cream = fat

Cheese = fat

Get the point?

Greasy cheeseburgers, extra-cheese pizza, potato chips . . .

So, I use a lot of olive oil in my cooking. It's fat, and whether people know it or not, people like fat.

CONSISTENCY

Consistency, consistency, consistency.

You can cook one hundred meals and get ninety-nine of them right, but the *one* you mess up is the one they will remember.

Timing, timing, timing.

Set yourself up to produce consistently great meals, and if something ever happens to go wrong—and it will—try to figure out how to prevent a repeat.

Having quick-fix backup plans is always a good idea.

I think I've made my mark as a dive boat chef, an Alaska fishing lodge chef, and a private chef by providing one thing over and over and over. Every meal, every day, every week, etc.

That one thing is that I continue to provide consistently great food every meal.

Consistency—work on it, develop it, have backup plans if something goes wrong.

—Chef Kevin

TASTING SPOONS/TASTING

Costco had/has a plastic spoon box—I think five hundred each. It might be one thousand, I can't remember.

I went through one box a week.

Tasting, tasting, tasting.

When I first started private chef jobs, I would taste and adjust everything.

I think everyone should taste everything before it goes to the guest table. It doesn't matter what it is—fruit, canned beans, pasta sauce—everything should be tasted by the chef.

As the chef, you are the last line of defense before the food goes to the guest. If for whatever reason something isn't servable, don't serve it. Period. No exceptions.

I bought a couple of different brands of jar oysters for Thanksgiving. I tasted one jar—they were fine. I dumped the other kind in, then tasted one from the next can—they were off. The taste was borderline acceptable, and the smell was not right. They were not due to expire for three more days.

I ended up swallowing the so-so one. I made the decision not to serve the oyster stuffing, and, yup, I got sick from the oyster. It took a while later, but I got sick.

So, I took one for the team—the guests.

If I had served it, twelve to fifteen plus hours later my twenty Thanksgiving guests would have come down with food poisoning from oysters. How bad would that have been for my chef reputation—or anyone's? That's a big meal, and a big deal to get it right.

Don't get complacent and think that you have cooked the same recipe one thousand times—taste it anyway. Something could have gone wrong.

I worked with a sous chef on the *Aqua Cat* in the Bahamas. I was the new chef, she was my sous chef, and when I gave my speech about tasting, she said she didn't because she didn't want to gain weight.

If for whatever reason you decide that tasting everything becomes unimportant, then get a new career.

THE COOLERS' TEMPERATURE

One of the first things that I do wherever I go is check the temps of all the cooler units. I find the best way to do this is to take your yellow digital thermometer and stick it into several items, such as a lemon, an onion, or a jar of mayo.

I personally like thirty-seven degrees. Thirty-eight is okay, but no higher. If you go below thirty-six, then you gamble with things freezing. If your equipment is not at thirty-seven, get it fixed/adjusted ASAP.

BUTTER

To be salted or not to be salted.

I like salt. So, I've always used salted butter. All of my recipes use salted butter.

I know—some people like unsalted butter. I will leave the option up to you.

SLACKING PROTEINS

Some people may argue this point. But over time, I have come to the conclusion that bringing protein (meats/seafood) up to room temp simply by placing on the counter one to four hours prior to cooking actually does help with the cooking process, as well as improves the final product outcome.

SHOPPING

If you are like me, even though I have a playbook (shopping list), I sometimes wander off the beaten path when I'm out shopping. It's okay if it is kept to a minimum—there's always room for a new product or new things to taste-test.

But think about this: Shopping takes time, and the more you don't stay focused on your shopping list, the more time slips away. Also space—the more new things you buy or things you don't need, the less space you have in your vehicle, kitchen cupboards, refrigerator, and freezer.

I'll give you a drastic example just to make a point.

I recently went to a new house, and I had a few days to make Thanksgiving dinner for twenty people. The cupboards were empty. No pantry, nothing.

I wrote a menu and made a shopping list for Thanksgiving.

As tempting as it was while I was shopping to get this and that, which I knew I would eventually use and need, I had to keep myself focused on the shopping list for the menu I was about to cook. Space-wise and timewise.

Sticking to the plan was the best way to go.

MIS EN PLACE
French for "Everything in Its Place"

Time, time, time.

Trust me, as a chef, time is not on your side. Time is not your friend. I didn't say timing isn't your friend—I said *time*.

I have often wished there was more time in a day, as I usually have a larger to-do list than I can get done—a wish list, in other words.

So, having said that, everything in its place has a critical step toward saving you some time.

The way I translate it best for me is: You should be able to find anything and everything from a pot to a pan to a spice to a can of beans, etc., with your eyes closed. Yes, blindfolded, you should be able to handpick everything in your kitchen—muscle memory.

By having a system to keep everything in its place, you end up saving yourself a chunk of time in the long run. Every second counts.

MUSCLE MEMORY

My days can be long—6:00 a.m. to 9:00 p.m. Oftentimes, my mind wanders off, even if it's just thinking what I'll be doing next. While doing what I'm currently doing, I am sometimes operating on autopilot. So, if something isn't where my muscle memory goes to grab it, then I've wasted time.

Even drawers with your utensils are so important to keep organized. You don't want to waste minutes every time you go looking for the peeler or a spatula or whatever. And to add to that, you don't need to add to your frustration level, blood pressure level, etc. The chef job is hard enough as it is in a perfect world. So, try to keep things on the path of perfection by keeping your *mis en place* in order.

BELOW DECK

I was not on the show *Below Deck*, but for a combined total of about three years I did the chef job on different dive boats. The show is not that different than reality.

I remember watching a chef who had been on the show before. He had come back and said he questioned his ability to be able to do it again, declaring: I'm about to do the hardest chef job in the world.

I would have to agree with him. I did the boat chef job, and I believe it to be the hardest chef job that exists. What I tell people is that if you can do that job, and do it well, then you can pretty much do any other job out there.

CLEAN, CLEAN, CLEAN

Clean as you go.

Do the dishes as you go.

Clean the floors as needed.

Take the trash out often.

Keep your uniform clean.

Clean your fridges and freezers weekly.

I've gone to several dive boats as a private chef, and I get that time is not our friend as a chef, but to not keep the kitchen clean is a nightmare.

I took over several restaurants in my restaurant management years, and most all needed a good spring cleaning, makeover, paint job, etc. Afterward, it was critical to maintain the cleaning program. Cleaning is the first thing to go downhill in any poorly run or managed business.

PRETEST EVERYTHING

I would advise every chef at every level to take time to test any dish that they have never made and/or served before.

For instance, as an example, I would not serve a new mac and cheese recipe without having made it a day or so before. And that goes for every new recipe that you come across.

Yes, you may get lucky and it comes out fine. But don't play with danger and risk the possibility that it doesn't turn out great. Remember, we only want to serve great food, not so-so food.

The only way that this can work, and I have done this myself, is if you plan on serving something you have never cooked before, just have a backup plan in place ready to go if something goes wrong. I can't tell you how many times I've had to use my backup plan. More than you know.

So, one more time for the record: pretest, pretest, pretest everything.

One of the things that has put me on the map in The Private Chef World is simply that, pretesting. By doing so, I know that I'm going to serve consistently great food time and time and time again.

I can't stress this concept enough. If you only do one thing in this book, do this religiously, and do it forever.

MODERN-DAY PLATING

I have no problem with everything looking great. I do have a problem with it if it takes away from the food being at its best when it's served.

I've never heard anyone walk away from a meal saying, "That was the best-looking meal I ever ate." Nobody says that. It's only the best if the food tastes and is the best. Not the way it looks.

To some degree I understand the statement. People eat with their eyes. But I can argue that if one dish of food looks amazing and tastes just so-so, and the dish next to it looks Plain Jane but tastes over-the-top amazing, then the winner is . . . no contest: the amazing-tasting food, not the amazing-looking food.

Do your best to manage both great food and good-looking food. But please, error on the side of the food being great.

BUDGETS

Just make sure that the place/people/business that you private chef for give(s) you the budget amount you need to serve the guest what they want. I have no problems with a budget, but it equals what your meal will be.

RECIPES

M*y base recipe book* only consists of my go-to, time-tested, guest-tested, crowd-pleasing recipes. No point in hanging onto a not-up-to-par-level recipe.

I created most of the recipes in this book on my own. On some occasions, I will Google a recipe, use the foundation of it, and then take it in my own direction.

I have taken some recipes from other cookbooks, magazines, or favorite chefs of mine, such as Emeril Lagasse. But, again, for the most part, my base recipe book consists of mostly my creations, or versions of them.

Sometimes a recipe will take me several times to get right, like my Bistro Burger. It took about six tries. If you get lucky, you might hit a home run on the first try of a recipe you are trying to create, such as with my White Bean Stuffing.

RECIPE FORMAT

As we speak, I am keeping a recipe book. It's a notebook, and it's handwritten.

Even though this now transfers to a typed, published book, I didn't want to lose the feeling that it's my cookbook that I use to cook for my guests. If you are one of my guests, then now you have my playbook in your hands so that you can make some of the food I cooked for you that you liked.

I'm giving out the keys to my success in the form of a cookbook for guests and chefs to enjoy. But just because you give someone the keys to drive a Formula 1 race car doesn't mean they can get it around the track as well as the pro race car owner of those keys. Given the sketched-out format of this cookbook, some of the recipes require a foundational amount of cooking skills to achieve a good outcome.

I kept the feel of my existing cookbook alive. I didn't provide you with step-by-step, hold-your-hand recipes. You kind of need to know how to go with it and make it work.

For example, take a soup recipe: If you take all of the ingredients, dump them in a pot, turn it on high, boil it for a while, and say it's done, you are not going to get the same result as if you knew and followed the known steps to soup cooking. That is, you would cook ingredients in increments along the way as you slowly added the other ingredients. Experienced cooks have come to know that ingredients need to be cooked in a certain order.

I wanted to leave the corporate, cookie-cutter recipe guidelines out of my book.

We are private chefs.

We are not corporate pawns.

We can do our own thing.

Like Emeril Lagasse says: I can do what I want because it's *my* show.

As a private chef it's your show.

Keep in mind that you have to follow rule number one, which is constantly provide your guests with great food.

LIST OF RECIPES

1   CHEF KEVIN'S MEATBALLS

Ingredients

3 lb Ground beef 91% lean

5 tbsp Chopped garlic

2 Eggs

1 Yellow onion ¼ inch diced

6 tsp Kosher salt

1 tsp Nutmeg

3 tsp Black pepper

2 tbsp Parsley

1 ½ cups Panko breadcrumbs

½ cup Italian breadcrumbs

1 cup Mozzarella cheese shredded

1 ¼ cups Sharp cheddar cheese
  shredded

½ cup H2O + ½ cup olive oil

#16 Scoop dinner size (2 oz each)
Purple scoop appetizer size

Instructions

1. Place formed meatballs on foil-lined sheet pan. Spray with pan spray. Put 1 cup H2O on meatballs.
2. 420 degree oven about 20 min.
3. 160 center temp.

Yield: about 20 people
Prep time: 40 min

Chef Kevin

2   BÉARNAISE SAUCE

Ingredients

1 ½ cup Butter	6 tsp Tarragon
6 tbsp Chopped red onion	Add 1 tbsp Kosher salt
6 tbsp Red wine vinegar	6 tsp Fresh chop curly parsley
12 Egg yolks	1 tsp Dry Coleman's mustard
12 tbsp Heavy cream	¼ tsp Cayenne
9 tsp Fresh lemon juice	

Instructions

1. Bring the above to a simmer, then temper in egg yolks.
2. Return to egg; set temp about 175.

Yield: about 20 people
Prep time: 30 min

Chef Kevin

3   CHIMICHURRI

Ingredients

6 cups Medium-packed Italian flat leaf parsley—cleaned, mostly leaves

8 tbsp Chopped garlic

12 tsp Oregano

¾ cup Red wine vinegar

7 tsp Kosher salt

1 ½ tsp Black pepper

1 ½ tsp Red pepper flakes

3 cups Olive oil

Instructions

Slowly blended into robo coup.

Yield: about 40 people

Prep time: 30 min

Chef Kevin

4   MUFFINS

Mix dry ingredients with a whisk thoroughly.

2 cups Flour	½ tsp Bake soda
¾ cup Quick oats or raw	¾ tsp Cinnamon
1 tsp Bake powder	¼ tsp Kosher salt

Separate bowl

1 cup Apple sauce	½ cup Half and Half
¼ cup Olive oil	1 ¼ cups Blueberries
1 ½ cups Sugar	½ cup Coconut flakes
1 Egg	½ cup Flakes, sprinkle on top

Instructions

375 oven about 15 min.

Yield: 12 muffins
Prep time: 30 min

Chef Kevin

5   COOKIES

Ingredients

½ cup Butter, soft not melted

¾ cup White sugar

½ cup Brown sugar

1 Egg

1 tsp Vanilla

1 tsp Bake soda (mix together with H2O)

2 tsp hot H2O

Separate bowl

1 ½ cups Flour

1 tbsp Cornstarch

½ tsp Kosher salt

1 cup Chips, any flavor

½ cup Heath bar crumbles

½ cup Oreo crumbles

Instructions

1. Oven—about 335.
2. About 13 min.

Yield: about 12 cookies

Prep time: 30 min

Chef Kevin

6   **HUMMUS**

Ingredients

2 cans Chickpeas, equal to 1 ¼ lbs
¾ cup Tahini
3 tbsp Chopped garlic
1 tsp Kosher salt

1 tsp Black pepper
1 tbsp Sambal oelek
2 Lemons juiced

Instructions

1. Slowly add 1 cup olive oil to the robo coup.
2. Blend to smooth.

Yield: about 20 people
Prep time: 25 min

Chef Kevin

7   CHUTNEY

Ingredients

3 tbsp Olive oil

1 ½ lbs Apricots ¼ inch diced

10 oz Dry cherries

1 cup Brown sugar

1 cup Apple cider vinegar

3 tbsp Pickled ginger

3 tbsp Chopped garlic in oil

1 tsp Kosher salt

1 tsp Black pepper

1 cup Orange juice

½ of Red onion ¼ inch diced

Instructions

Cook on lowest heat. Simmer for about 1 hour.

Yield: about 20 people

Prep time: 25 min

Chef Kevin

8   APPLE OR BLUEBERRY CRISP

Ingredients

8 oz Butter softened	1 cup Sugar
2 cups Flour	½ cup Oats raw

Mix above together. This is the topping.

Separate bowl:

Approx. 10 apples peeled and sliced thin	1 cup Raisins
Or Blueberries—fill pan, then dump into a bowl	1 cup Sugar
	2 tsp Cinnamon
3 Limes juiced	1 tsp Allspice
3–5 tbsp Cornstarch	1 tsp Nutmeg

Instructions

Bake 375 for 45 min.

Yield: about 20 people
Prep time: 30 min

Chef Kevin

9   COCONUT RICE

Ingredients

1 can Coconut milk, then add
   H2O until total liquid equals 8
   ½ cups
1 tbsp Kosher salt

1 cup Coconut flakes
5 tbsp Olive oil
5 cups Jasmine Rice

Instructions

1. Bring to boil—set 5 min timer. Then turn to med-low heat—set 7 min timer.
2. About 12 total min cook time.

Yield: about 20 people
Prep time: 20 min

Chef Kevin

10   CLUB CAR OLIVE TAPENADE

Ingredients

5 oz Green olives

5 oz Kalamata olives

5 oz Black olives

1 oz Chopped garlic

½ tsp Sambal oelek

½ tsp Black pepper

½ tsp Kosher salt

¼ oz Fresh parsley

1 Lemon juiced

2 oz Roasted red peppers

½ tsp Red pepper flakes

2 tsp Kosher salt

Instructions

1. Mix in robo coup.
2. Add olive oil slowly until you reach the smoothness you want.

Yield: about 20 people

Prep time: 15 min

Chef Kevin

11   GUACAMOLE

Ingredients

10 Ripe avocados

1 pint Grape tomatoes ¼ cut

¼ of Red onion ⅛ inch diced

3 Green onion ⅛ sliced

1 bunch Cilantro chopped

2 tbsp Chopped garlic

4 tbsp Olive oil

1 ½ tsp Black pepper

2 tsp Kosher salt

4–6 Limes juiced

Instructions

Mix together—leave chunky style

Yield: about 20 people

Prep time: 35 min

Chef Kevin

12   MACARONI SALAD

Ingredients

1 lb Elbow pasta

3 cups Kosher salt

½ cup White onion ⅛ inch diced

½ cup Carrots shredded

2 cups Mayo

1 tsp White pepper

2 tsp Kosher salt

Instructions

1. Cook pasta in boiling salted H2O for 12 min.
2. Cool pasta under cold H2O.
3. Mix pasta and remaining ingredients.

Yield: about 10 people

Prep time: 30 min

Chef Kevin

13 GREEK DRESSING

Ingredients

1 cup Red wine vinegar

5 Fresh lemons juiced

2 tbsp Oregano

3 tsp Kosher salt

2 tsp Black pepper

4 tbsp Chopped garlic

2 tbsp Dijon mustard

2 tsp Garlic salt

2 cups Olive oil, add to blender
  slowly

Yield: about 20 people

Prep time: 20 min

Chef Kevin

14 ROASTED RED PEPPER SAUCE

Ingredients

3 tbsp Olive oil

1 Red onion ¼ inch diced

3 tbsp Chopped garlic

16 oz Roasted red peppers

1 cup Red wine

3 cups H2O warm

2 tbsp Tomato bullion

Instructions

1. Cook above in saucepan. Use blender stick to blend to slightly chunky.
2. Add cornstarch slurry to thicken.
3. Lastly, add 4 oz salted butter.

Yield: 20 people

Prep time: 30 min

Chef Kevin

15   BANANA BREAD

Ingredients

4 Ripe bananas
1 cup Sugar
½ cup Applesauce

1 tsp Vanilla
2 Eggs

Separate bowl
1 tsp Bake soda
1 tsp Bake powder
1 tsp Kosher salt

2 cups Flour
1 cup Coconut flakes

Instructions

1. Combine both bowls of separately mixed items. Divide into two bread pans.
2. 350 oven for 45 min.
3. Toothpick clean test.

Yield: 20 loaves (20 people)
Prep time: 20 min

Chef Kevin

16 LEMON CAPER PICCATA SAUCE

Ingredients

4 tbsp Olive oil

1 Yellow onion ¼ inch diced

⅓ cup Capers

2 tbsp Chopped garlic

2 Lemons juiced

1 cup White wine

Reduce wine by half simmer.

3 cups H2O—make a chicken stock, slightly strong Cornstarch slurry to thicken

½ tsp Kosher salt

½ tsp Black pepper

1 each 4 oz Stick butter (add just before service)

½ cup Heavy cream (add just before service)

Yield: 20 people

Prep time: 35 min

Chef Kevin

17   SEARED AHI TUNA SALAD

Ingredients

About 2 lbs Ahi tuna seared, diced
   ¼ inch cubes
1 cup Mayo—more if needed
1 Fresh jalapeño ¼ inch diced
1 tbsp Chopped garlic
2 tbsp Olive oil
½ tsp Black pepper
½ tsp Kosher salt

1 Lime juiced
¼ cup Fresh parsley chopped
¼ cup Cilantro chopped
¼ Red bell pepper ¼ inch diced
1 stalk Celery ¼ inch diced
⅛ of Red onion ⅛ inch diced
2 Green onions ⅛ inch sliced

Instructions

1. Mix above together.
2. Leave chunky style.

Yield: about 10 people
Prep time: 30 min

Chef Kevin

18   CHICKEN POSOLE SOUP

Ingredients

4 tbsp Olive oil

3 stalks Celery ¼ inch diced

1 Carrot ¼ inch diced

1 Yellow onion ¼ inch diced

5 tbsp Chopped garlic

25 oz can Hominy with juice

1 bunch Cilantro rough chop

2 tbsp Cumin

1 tbsp Oregano

2 ½ cups Cooked chicken diced

4 Limes juiced

3 qt Warm H2O—make into
a chicken stock with base

2 tbsp Sambal oelek

Instructions

Thicken with a cornstarch slurry.

Yield: about 20 people

Prep time: 45 min

Chef Kevin

19   SMOKED SALMON MARINADE

Ingredients

4 qt Cold H2O
1 ½ cups Kosher salt

4 cups Brown sugar
½ cup Liquid smoke

Instructions

1. Mix above together.
2. Debone 5 whole salmon filets.
3. Submerge in liquid.
4. Marinate 1–2 days.
5. Traeger—180 about 2 hours.
6. Done at 110.

Yield: about 40 people
Prep time: 30 min

Chef Kevin

20   SMOKED SALMON DIP

Ingredients

1 ½ lbs Cream cheese, room temp   1 lb Sour cream

Mix above together in a mixer w/paddle.

¼ cup Chopped garlic—sauteed or   ¼ cup Cajun seasoning
    use roasted garlic   1 cup Green onions sliced
2 cups Shredded Parmesan cheese   1 ½ tbsp Kosher salt

Instructions

1. Blend above together.
2. Add 1 ½ lbs Smoked salmon, rough chop
3. Can serve cold or warm.

Yield: about 40 people
Prep time: 30 min

Chef Kevin

21   KEY LIME PIE

Ingredients

2 10 inch Graham cracker pie   1 cup Cream cheese
   shells   1 cup Fresh lime juice
3 cans Sweetened condensed milk   3 Eggs

Instructions

1. Blend in blender to smooth.
2. 325 for 25 min until it jiggles firm, up to 30 min if needed. Do not
    overcook.

Yield: 2 pies (16 people)
Prep time: 20 min

Chef Kevin

22   COOKIE PIE

Ingredients

1 cup Butter   2 Eggs
1 cup Brown sugar   1 tbsp Vanilla
1 cup White sugar

Separate bowl
3 cups Flour   1 ½ tsp Bake powder
1 ½ tsp Kosher salt   1 lb White chocolate chips

Instructions

1. Best cooked in a cast iron skillet pan.
2. 325 for about 45 min—golden brown on top.

Yield: 8–12 people
Prep time: 30 min

Chef Kevin

23   AHI POKE

Ingredients

1 ½ lbs Raw ahi tuna ¼–½ inch diced

¼ of Red onion ⅛ inch diced

½ of Cucumber seeded and ¼ inch diced

1 Avocado

3 Green onions ⅛ inch sliced

4 tbsp Olive oil

2 tbsp Soy sauce

2 tbsp Sesame oil

1 tsp Kosher salt

1 tsp Black pepper

1 tbsp Sambal oelek

Yield: 20 people

Prep time: 15 min

Chef Kevin

24   CRÈME BRÛLÉE

Ingredients

1 qt Heavy cream	1 cup White chocolate chips
1 can Coconut milk	1 cup Coconut flakes

Bring on med-low heat up to 140, stirring frequently. Do not go over 140.

10 Egg yolks whipped	1 tsp Coconut extract
¾ cups Sugar	1 tsp Vanilla extract

Instructions

1. Temper in egg mixture.
2. Place in crème brûlée cups.
3. About 4 oz each.
4. Water bath pan.
5. 325 for 30–45 min.
6. Eggs set at 175.
7. Do not go over temp.

Yield: 14 people
Prep time: 35 min

Chef Kevin

25   COCONUT MACAROONS

Ingredients

1 ¾ lbs Sweetened coconut flakes	¾ cups Flour

Mix above thoroughly.

1 can Sweetened condensed milk	½ cup Heath bar crunch
1 tsp Vanilla	½ cup White chocolate chips

Instructions

1. Mix above all together.
2. Roll into golf ball size.
3. 325 for 25 min.
4. Also use mixture to line graham cracker crust pans for coconut crème pie.

Yield: 20 people
Prep time: 30 min

Chef Kevin

26   COCONUT CRÈME PIE

Ingredients

2 10-inch Graham cracker pie shells
Use half of the recipe of Coconut Macaroons—line pie shells with ¼ inch macaroon. Bake 325 for 20 min.

Mix together the following:

4 Egg yolks   ¼ cup Cornstarch

Simmer the following to about 175–180

1 can Coconut milk   ½ tsp Kosher salt
1 cup Half and half   1 cup Coconut flakes
⅔ cups Sugar

Instructions

1. Add egg and cornstarch, return to 175–180. Remove from heat.
2. Add 2 tbsp butter
3. 1 tsp Vanilla
4. 1 tsp Coconut extract
5. Put mix into pie shells—cool in fridge.

Yield: 16 people
Prep time: 35 min

Chef Kevin

27   GRATIN POTATOES

Ingredients

Large roasting pan—pan spray
3 qt Heavy cream
3 tbsp Rosemary
3 tbsp Chopped garlic

7 tbsp Kosher salt
About 20–25 Russet potatoes,
    peeled and sliced ⅛ inch

Instructions

1. Place sliced potatoes in roasting pan.
2. Bring above cream mix to 140—do not go over. Pour 140 cream on potatoes.
3. 350 oven, cover with foil—cook 1 hour. Remove foil—cook about another ½ hour until top is golden brown and potatoes are tender.

Yield: about 40 people
Prep time: 60 min

Chef Kevin

28   CREAM CHEESE FROSTING

Ingredients

8 oz Cream cheese

½ tsp Vanilla

¼ cup H2O

5 cups Powdered sugar

¼ stick Butter (2 tbsp)—melted

Instructions

Mix in mixer.

Yield: 40+ people

Prep time: 15 min

Chef Kevin

29   FOCACCIA BREAD

Ingredients

2 ⅔ cups Warm H2O 110 or less. Over 110 kills yeast.

4 tsp Active dry yeast

7 cups Flour

½ cup Olive oil

4 tsp Kosher salt

1 tbsp Rosemary

Instructions

1. Rise in bowl 1 hour.
2. Push down—put in bread pans or sheet tray.
3. Rise 1 more hour.
4. 375 for about 12–15 min.

Yield: 40 people

Prep time: 30 min

Chef Kevin

30   WALDORF DRESSING

Ingredients

2 cups Mayo

2 cups Greek yogurt

2 tbsp Chopped garlic

½ cup Fresh lime juice

4 tsp Kosher salt

3 tsp Black pepper

Instructions

Mix above together.

Yield: 4 ½ cups (about 20 people)

Prep time: 15 min

Chef Kevin

31   BUFFALO CHICKEN DIP

Ingredients

2 ½ cups Cream cheese

2 ½ cups Sour cream

2 ½ cups Shredded Jack cheddar

5 cups Cooked sous vide chicken ¼ inch diced

1 ½ cups Frank's RedHot

Instructions

1. Mix above together.
2. Bring up to 140 very slowly—like in a warmer or chafe dish on low setting. Hover at 140 to serve. Serve with tortilla chips.

Yield: about 40 people

Prep time: 30 min

Chef Kevin

32   BISTRO BURGER

Ingredients

5 lbs 73/27 Fat ground beef or use   2 ½ tbsp Chopped garlic
    Wagyu ground   ¾ tsp Cayenne
2 ½ tsp Black pepper   2 ½ tsp Granulated onion

Instructions

1. Portion into 2 oz balls. Place between two sheets of wax paper—
    smash with sauté pan to ¼ inch thick. Season both sides with Kosher
    salt just before cooking.
2. Place on a 350 griddle and cook until juices surface. Flip.
3. Place American cheese on top side, melt, and remove. Three patties
    per burger bun, each patty placed 25% on top of the next one in a
    circle pattern so that with some bites, the guest gets a triple-layer bite.
    Overlay buttered toasted brioche bun, bacon bits, mayo, lettuce,
    and tomato.

Yield: 13 burgers
Prep time: 45 min

Chef Kevin

33   HOMINY GRITS

Ingredients

½ lb Pancetta or bacon
4 tbsp Olive oil
½ lb Yellow onion
4 Green onions
1 Fresh jalapeño
1 cup Canned corn
½ cup White wine

2 Limes juiced
2 tsp Kosher salt
1 tsp Black pepper
1 cup Cilantro rough chop
5 cups Hominy
8 oz Fontina cheese shredded

Instructions

1. Cook down above ingredients on medium heat.
2. Use hand stick blender to mix—leave chunky.
3. Serve warm—with shrimp.

Yield: 40 people
Prep time: 30 min

Chef Kevin

34   SWEET AND SOUR SAUCE

Ingredients

½ cup Brown sugar

½ cup Rice vinegar

½ cup Ketchup

1 tbsp Soy sauce

1 Pineapple blended

1 tbsp Cornstarch

1 Red bell pepper ½ inch diced

1 cup Pineapple ½ inch diced

1 bunch Green onions sliced

Instructions

1. Cook on medium/low heat until sauce thickens.
2. Serve with appetizer meatballs.

Yield: about 40 people

Prep time: 30 min

Chef Kevin

35   ASIAN DRESSING #1

Ingredients

1 cup Mae ploy

3 oz Fresh peeled grated ginger
    root

⅔ cup Dijon mustard

½ cup Soy sauce

½ cup Rice vinegar

6 tbsp Chopped garlic

1 bunch Green onions

Instructions

Add 1 ½ cups olive oil slowly to the blender. Blend to smooth.

Yield: about 20 people

Prep time: 20 min

Chef Kevin

36   CREAM OF MUSHROOM SOUP

Ingredients

4 tbsp Olive oil

1 Yellow onion ¼ inch diced

3 Stalks celery ¼ inch diced

1 Carrot ¼ inch diced

1 tsp Kosher salt

1 tsp Black pepper

4 tbsp Chopped garlic

3 qt H2O—make into a chicken base/stock

About 2 lbs Portobello mushrooms cleaned and ½ inch diced

Instructions

1. Set blender to slight chunky. Slurry to thicken.
2. Before service add:

1 each 4 oz Stick butter   3 cups Heavy cream

Yield: 20 people

Prep time: 30 min

Chef Kevin

37   HALIBUT OLYMPIA

Skin halibut, then season both sides with Kosher salt and black pepper. About 10 yellow onions Julianne cut. Mix in bowl with:

1 cup Olive oil   1 tbsp Black pepper
2 tbsp Kosher salt

350 oven about 20 min. Cook to golden brown. Cool onions. When the cooked onions have cooled, take ¼ inch slices of a stick of butter and place them evenly on top of the onions. Spread out on sheet trays. The seasoned halibut then sits on top of the butter and onions.

Topping
2 ½ cups Mayo   1 tbsp Kosher salt
2 ½ cups Sour cream   1 tbsp Black pepper
3 tbsp Dill

Top halibut with ¼ inch of sour cream mixture. Sprinkle with Panko breadcrumbs. 425 oven—about 6–7 min. Pull out when center temp is about 90. Cover 10 min. Check temp. Center perfect is 110.

Yield: 40 people
Prep time: 90 min

Chef Kevin

38   SEAFOOD FRITTERS

Ingredients
2 cans Corn (22 ½ oz) and/or fresh

½ lb Miscellaneous seafood plus 1 lb crab meat—can or fresh (or a total of 1 ½ lb seafood combined)

Mix Dry
2 cups Flour
1 tbsp Bake powder
3 tsp Sugar

2 tsp Kosher salt
¼ tsp Cayenne

Mix Wet
1 cup Milk
3 Eggs
1 tbsp Tabasco
1 tbsp Worcestershire sauce
2 cups Mayo
1 Lime juiced

3 Green onions sliced ⅛ inch
1 tbsp Chili powder
1 tbsp Garlic
1 tsp Black pepper
1 tsp Kosher salt

Instructions
1. Golf ball size scoop.
2. Fryer 350. Center temp 160.

Yield: 20 people
Prep time: 30 min

Chef Kevin

39   CEVICHE

Ingredients

1 ½ lbs Raw seafood (Mahi fresh works great)

1 Tomato ¼ inch diced

½ cup Cilantro

1 Fresh jalapeño ⅛ inch diced

1 tbsp Chopped garlic

½ cup Lime juice

½ cup Lemon juice

1 tsp Kosher salt

½ cup Mandarin orange juice from can—toss in the Mandarin oranges as well

1 tsp Siracha

2 Avocados ½–¼ diced

Instructions

1. Mix above together.
2. Add seafood 1 hour before service.

Yield: about 20 people

Prep time: 40 min

Chef Kevin

40   KEVIN'S WHITE BEAN STUFFING

Ingredients

1 lb Chorizo

1 lb Andouille ¼ inch diced

1 lb Pancetta ¼ inch diced

Sauté the above to 95 percent almost cooked.

2 Yellow onions ¼ inch diced

½ lb Carrots ¼ inch diced

1 lb Celery ¼ inch diced

Sauté the above with meats.

About 2 lbs sourdough or similar bread ½ inch cubes

16 oz Hot H2O—make into a strong chicken base with 1 tbsp chicken base paste

1 one each number 10 can Great northern beans, equivalent to 12 ¾ cups of beans

1 tbsp Kosher salt

1 tbsp Black pepper

¾ lb Butter

Sauté above together.

Yield: 40 people

Prep time: 50 min

Chef Kevin

41   BBQ RIBS APPETIZER/DINNER

Remove membrane from baby back ribs. Cut off the excess meat that usually dries out. Leave the center strip. Shave the excess meat off parallel to the ribs. You only want the meat between the ribs. Brine over night—see Brine recipe.

Use 1 gallon H2O to 1 cup Kosher salt.

Kosher salt and black pepper both sides of the ribs.

Put in pan, cover tightly with foil.

Bake 300 for about 2 hours, more if needed. Should be able to pinch your fingers together on the meat.

If it's rubber band-like, continue to cook until tender.

Yield: 40 people
Prep time: 15 to 60 min

Chef Kevin

A Side Note on BBQ Ribs
1. They have about a 15- to 20-minute window.
2. Less than the window, the ribs will be tough and chewy.
3. Go over the 15- to 20-minute sweet spot and you have mush.
4. Once the ribs are done, cool.
5. Reheat in oven to serve.

42   REMOULADE SAUCE

Ingredients

3 cups Mayo
3 tbsp Smoked paprika
½ cup Chopped parsley
1 tbsp Cajun seasoning
¼ cup Dill relish
1 tbsp Frank's RedHot
2 tbsp Chopped garlic
1 tbsp Black pepper

½ cup Cilantro chopped
¼ cup Chives
2 Limes juiced
¼ cup Sliced green onions
1 tbsp Kosher salt
¼ cup Olive oil
¼ cup Capers

Yield: about 1 quart (40 people)
Prep time: 30 min

Chef Kevin

43   CHICKEN MARINADE

Ingredients

10 tbsp Olive oil

5 tbsp Sesame oil

1 cup Soy sauce

5 tbsp Worcestershire sauce

3 Lemons juiced

3 Limes juiced

1 cup Maple syrup

1 cup Chopped garlic

2 tbsp Black pepper

5 tbsp Kosher salt

Instructions

1. Mix above together.
2. Marinate chicken overnight.

Yield: about 10 lbs chicken (30+ people)

Prep time: 20 min

Chef Kevin

44   BROWN RICE WITH MANGO

Ingredients

Large 5 gallon pot   1 ½ cups Kosher salt
¾ full H2O

Instructions

1. Yield equals ⅓ cup raw rice per person.
2. Turn on high to bring to a boil. Total simmer time about 40–45 min.
3. Rinse, cool.
4. Reheat on flat top with olive oil, Kosher salt, black pepper, and mango.

Yield: 40 people
Prep time: 15 min

Chef Kevin

45   SHRIMP EGG ROLLS/RICE PAPERS

Ingredients

1 bunch Green onions
½ Yellow onions sliced
1 Large carrot shredded
½ head White cabbage sliced

1 tbsp Chicken base
2 tsp Kosher salt
1 tsp Black pepper

Sauté above.

1 ¾ lbs Raw shrimp rough chop
1 tsp Kosher salt
1 tsp Black pepper

1 tsp Paprika
1 tsp Granulated garlic
1 tbsp Sambal oelek

Sauté above.

Mix both together in sauté pan. Add 5 whole eggs. Cook until just done, then cool a bit. Add mixture to egg rolls or rice papers.

Yield: 20+ people
Prep time: 40 min

Chef Kevin

46   CILANTRO LIME DRESSING

Ingredients

5 cups Mayo

5 tbsp Dry cilantro

5 tbsp Chopped garlic

5 Limes juiced

5 tsp Kosher salt

1 ¼ cups Olive oil

Instructions

Mix above together.

Yield: 40 people

Prep time: 20 min

Chef Kevin

47   BEEF TIPS MARINADE

Ingredients

1 cup Olive oil
⅔ cup Soy sauce
2 Lemons juiced
½ cup Worcestershire sauce
2 tbsp Garlic powder

2 tbsp Italian seasoning
2 tsp Black pepper
2 tsp Kosher salt
2 tsp Tabasco

Yield: 2 cups (40 people)
Prep time: 10 min

Chef Kevin

- Use 1 inch meat cubes
- Filet mignon, prime rib, etc.
- Only marinate for 2–4 hours. It's a strong marinade. Any longer and the meat starts to cook.

48 THOUSAND ISLAND CHIPOTLE DRESSING

Ingredients

3 cups Mayo
14 oz Ketchup
1 cup Dill relish
1 cup Sweet relish
4 tbsp Chipotle adobe sauce

½ cup Chopped garlic
2 tbsp Kosher salt
1 tbsp Black pepper
1 tsp Tabasco

Instructions

Mix above together with wisp.

Yield: about 30 Lobster Louie Salads
Prep time: 20 min

Chef Kevin

49   HOUSE COCKTAIL SAUCE

Ingredients

5 cups Chili sauce

4 cups Ketchup

1 cup Horseradish

¾ cup Fresh lemon juice

5 tsp Worcestershire sauce

3 tsp Tabasco

Instructions

Mix above together.

Yield: 11 cups (88 oz) (40 people)

Prep time: 25 min

Chef Kevin

50   KEVIN'S MAC AND CHEESE

Ingredients

3 lbs Elbow pasta

5 gallon pot—¾ full H2O

3 cups Kosher salt—7 min cook
time

Cool pasta to room temp.

6 oz Flour

6 oz Butter

3 tbsp Olive oil

3 tbsp Kosher salt

6 tsp Chicken base paste

3 cups Heavy cream

6 cups Half and Half

Bring above to 140, then add cheese.

36 oz Fontina shredded   18 oz Shredded cheddar

Add this second amount of half and half to the cooled pasta:

3 cups Half and Half

Then add warm cheese mix to the pasta.

Mix everything together. Put in a sprayed pan, then cover with foil. Bake 350 about 1 hour.

Center temp—140 goal.

Yield: 30 people

Prep time: 60 min

Chef Kevin

51   CRAB CAKES

Ingredients

1 Egg	1 tsp Old Bay
¼ cup Mayo	2 tsp Lemon juice
1 tbsp Fresh chopped parsley	½ tsp Kosher salt
2 tsp Dijon mustard	1 lb Crabmeat
2 tsp Worcestershire sauce	⅔ cup Crushed saltines

Instructions

1. Mix above together, adding crab last. Try to fold in, keeping crabmeat as together as possible. Mold into golf ball-size portions—brush with melted butter.
2. 450, 12–15 min.
3. Serve with Joe's mustard sauce.

Yield: about 15 crab cakes (10 people)
Prep time: 30 min

Chef Kevin

52   GREEK YOGURT CHICKEN

Ingredients

32 oz Greek plain yogurt   5 tbsp Black pepper
5 tbsp Kosher salt   1 cup Chopped garlic

Mix above together.

Instructions

1. About 10 lbs raw chicken.
2. Marinate overnight.
3. Cook 300, about 30 min.
4. Different cuts of chicken have different done temps.

Yield: 20–40 people
Prep time: 30 min

Chef Kevin

53   CREAM CHEESE EGG ROLLS

Ingredients

3 lbs Cooked seafood, such as crab-   1 ½ lbs Cream cheese
meat, etc.   1 tsp Kosher salt
½ lb Mozzarella shredded   1 tsp Black pepper

Instructions

1. Mix above together.
2. Stuff egg roll wrappers.
3. Egg wash sides to seal.
4. Fry in fryer to golden brown.

Yield: 40 people
Prep time: 45 min

Chef Kevin

54   BLENDER HOLLANDAISE

Ingredients

12 Egg yolks

4 tbsp Fresh lemon juice

1 tsp Dijon mustard

4 dashes Tabasco

2 cups Melted butter

Instructions

1. Mix above 4 ingredients together in blender. Slowly add butter.
2. Adjust with H2O, more flavor if desired.
3. Adjust with water if necessary. Also add more salt, lemon, hot sauce depending on what flavor you want.
4. Keep warm until service.
5. Do not overheat.
6. Keep below 130.

Yield: 20 people

Prep time: 20 min

Chef Kevin

55   JEN'S HOMEMADE BREAD

Ingredients

2 cups Warm H2O (110 or less)   ¼ cup Olive oil
⅔ cup Sugar   6 cups Bread flour
1 ½ tbsp Yeast   1 tbsp Rosemary
1 ½ tsp Kosher salt   1 tbsp Chopped garlic

Instructions

1. Rise 1 hour in ball form.
2. Mold into bake pans.
3. Rise 1 hour.
4. Bake 350 about 15–20 min.

Yield: 40 people
Prep time: 20 min

Chef Kevin

56 JOE'S STONE CRAB MUSTARD SAUCE

Ingredients

3 ½ tsp Coleman's dry mustard

1 cup Mayo

2 tsp Worcestershire sauce

1 tsp A.1. steak sauce

¼ tsp Kosher salt

2 tbsp Heavy cream

Instructions

Mix above together.

Yield: 10 people

Prep time: 15 min

Chef Kevin

57   FALAFEL

Ingredients

1 can Garbanzo beans	3 tbsp Chopped garlic
½ Yellow onion ¼ inch diced	1 tsp Cumin
2 tbsp Fresh parsley	1 tsp Bake powder
2 tbsp Fresh cilantro	4–6 tsp Flour
1 tsp Kosher salt	If non-vegan—add 1 egg for
½ tsp Hot pepper flakes	a binder

Instructions

1. Mix above together.
2. Form into burger-size patties.
3. Sear both sides. Finish in oven to 180.
4. Serve with tzatziki sauce.

Yield: 4–6 burgers
Prep time: 30 min

Chef Kevin

58 KEVIN'S STUFFED SHELLS

Ingredients

1 package Large jumbo shells
  (Cook in salt H2O for 9 min,
  then cool.)
1 Red onion ¼ inch diced
½ tsp Kosher salt
½ tsp Black pepper

5 tbsp Chopped garlic
4 tbsp Olive oil
2 cups Broccoli chopped
2 cups Spinach chopped
1 cup Asparagus chopped

Sauté above to tender.

7 ½ oz Ricotta cheese
2 eggs
2 ½ cups Shredded mozzarella

½ cup Grated Parmesan
2 cups Mixed Jack cheddar shred

Instructions

1. Add above cheese mix to slightly cooled sautéed mixture.
2. Stuff shells with mix. Line bake pan with ½ inch marinara and put
    shells on marinara. Drizzle top with marinara plus Alfredo sauce.
3. 350, 1 hour—center temp 140.

Yield: 20 people
Prep time: 45 min

Chef Kevin

59   KING FISHER CLAM CHOWDER

Ingredients

3 cans Clams—separate juice

4 cans Clam juice—make with clam base

4 tbsp Kosher salt

6 qt ½ inch Diced potatoes cooked in salted H2O about 8 min al dente

1 lb Raw bacon ¼ inch diced

¼ cup Olive oil

2 qt ½ inch Diced celery

1 ½ qt Yellow onion ½ inch diced

Add 2 tbsp to above sautéed—Kosher salt

2 cups White wine—reduce

1 ¼ lbs Butter

1 ¼ lbs Flour—make roux

Instructions

1. Add 140 heated clam juice.
2. 1 ½ qt Heavy cream
3. Add cooked potatoes and clams.
4. 2 tbsp Thyme—to sauté veggies

Yield: 4 gallons

Prep time: 60 min

Chef Kevin

60   BAKED POTATO SALAD

Ingredients

2 qt Cooked russet potatoes

¼ of a Red onion ⅛ inch diced

2 Green onions sliced

2 tbsp Sweet relish

1 tbsp Dijon mustard

2 tbsp Chopped garlic

1 tsp Sambal oelek

1 tsp Kosher salt

1 tsp Black pepper

¾ cup Mayo—more if needed

3 tbsp Olive tapenade or sub-chopped green olives

2 tbsp White vinegar

1 stalk Celery ¼ inch diced

¼ of a Red bell pepper ¼ inch diced

2 tbsp Dry parsley

½ cup Bacon bits

1 tsp Smoked paprika

Yield: 20 people

Prep time: 30 min

Chef Kevin

61   TZATZIKI

Ingredients

10 oz Greek yogurt plain
4 oz Seeded ¼ inch diced
   cucumber
1 tsp Kosher salt
1 tsp Black pepper
1 tsp Chopped garlic

1 oz ⅛ inch Diced red onion
1 tbsp Fresh lemon juice
1 tbsp Olive oil
⅛ tsp Cayenne
¼ oz Fresh dill or 1 tbsp dry

Instructions

1. Mix above together.
2. Season more if needed.

Yield: 20 people
Prep time: 20 min

Chef Kevin

62   BLACK BEAN HUMMUS

Ingredients

1 can Black beans drained

2 Limes juiced

1 tbsp Sambal oelek

1 tsp Chopped garlic

1 Fresh jalapeño ⅛ inch diced

1 oz Red onion ¼ inch diced

2 tsp Kosher salt

1 tsp Black pepper

1 tsp Oregano

½ oz Green onion sliced

Instructions

1. Robo coup to smooth.
2. Add a splash of olive oil if needed.

Yield: 20 people

Prep time: 25 min

Chef Kevin

63   CLUB CAR CHILI

Ingredients

4 oz Olive oil	2 Limes juiced
1 lb Ground beef	3 tbsp Chopped garlic
4 tsp Kosher salt	24 oz Beer
4 tsp Black pepper	6 cups Fire-roasted salsa
1 lb Yellow onion ½ inch diced	6 cups Crushed tomatoes
½ lb Red onion ½ inch diced	12 cups Black beans drained
½ lb Red bell pepper ½ inch diced	3 cups Black coffee
3 cups Fire-roasted corn	3 tbsp Chili powder
5 oz Fresh jalapeño ¼ inch diced	1 tbsp Cumin
2 oz Olive oil	1 tbsp Garlic salt

Yield: about 2 gallons (20+ people)
Prep time: 45 min

Chef Kevin

64   **BLACK BEAN SOUP**

Ingredients

5 tbsp Olive oil

1 Fresh jalapeño

3 stalks Celery ¼ inch diced

1 cup Red onion ¼ inch diced

2 oz Chopped cilantro (1 bunch)

1 cup Green onions

3 Limes juiced

1 can Refried beans

3 cans Black beans drained

3 qt Chicken base

Instructions

Slurry to thicken.

Yield: 20 people

Prep time: 45 min

Chef Kevin

65   BUTTER CAKE

Ingredients

¾ lb Butter room temp   1 tsp Kosher salt

2 cups Sugar   1 cup Milk room temp

6 Eggs room temp   2 tsp Vanilla

3 cups Flour   ½ cup Powdered sugar

4 tsp Bake powder   2 tbsp Milk

Instructions

1. 350 oven, 10 inch bun pan.
2. Mix butter and sugar to fluffy.
3. Add eggs one at a time.
4. Add premixed dry ingredients to mixer and slowly add milk.
5. Bake 60–80 min.
6. Toothpick done.
7. Powdered sugar, milk, vanilla is the frosting, plus sliced strawberries.

Yield: 20 people

Prep time: 30 min

Chef Kevin

66   BASIC CORN CHOWDER

Ingredients

1 Yellow onion ¼ inch diced

1 Carrot ¼ inch diced

3 stalks Celery

5 tbsp Chopped garlic

4 tbsp Olive oil

2 cans Corn with juice

3 qt Chicken base

1 qt Cooked potatoes ½ inch diced

2 tbsp Parsley

2 cups Mexi shredded cheese

½ stick (4 tbsp) Butter

2 cups Heavy cream

Yield: 20 people

Prep time: 45 min

Chef Kevin

67   KEVIN'S HOUSE POPCORN

Ingredients

Orville Redenbacher original   ¾ cup Corn kernels
    corn kernels   1 ¼ cups Olive oil

Instructions

1. Cook on high heat in 2 gallon pot with lid.
2. Season with Himalayan pink salt and sprinkle with grated Parmesan cheese.
3. Sometimes add truffle oil.
4. Siracha, BBQ sauce.

Yield: 20 people
Prep time: 20 min

Chef Kevin

68   OREO COOKIE BARS

Ingredients

2 cups Mini marshmallows   8 cups White chocolate chips
6 cups Oreo pieces

Instructions

1. Melt chocolate in a double-boil setup.
2. Add other ingredients.
3. Mix together.
4. Put in sprayed bake dish.
5. Cool, cut, serve.

Yield: 20 people
Prep time: 30 min

Chef Kevin

69   SCALLOP MORNAY SAUCE

Ingredients

8 tbsp Butter

1 Red onion ⅛ diced

6 Portobello mushrooms
   pre-sautéed

4 tbsp Kosher salt

1 tbsp White pepper

4 cups White wine—reduce by ½

4 cups Heavy cream

12 Egg yolks

1 tbsp Smoked paprika

½ tsp Cayenne

8 tsp Tarragon

2 Lemons juiced and zested

2 lbs Gruyere shredded

Yield: 40 people

Prep time: 45 min

Chef Kevin

70   ASIAN DRESSING #2

Ingredients

1 ½ cups Olive oil
1 ½ cups Rice vinegar
¾ cup Honey
1 cup Sesame oil

5 tbsp Soy sauce
1 tsp Kosher salt
5 tbsp Chopped garlic
4 oz Fresh ginger grated

Yield: 20 people
Prep time: 15 min

Chef Kevin

71   HOMEMADE TARRAGON RANCH DRESSING

Ingredients

4 tbsp Chopped garlic

3 tbsp Kosher salt

4 cups Mayo

2 cups Sour cream

2 cups Half and half—mix with 2 lemons or use buttermilk

⅔ cup Tarragon

½ cup Parsley

½ cup White vinegar

¼ cup Worcestershire sauce

2 tbsp Black pepper

1 tsp Tabasco

2 tbsp Onion powder

1 tbsp Garlic salt

Yield: 2 ½ qt (about 40 people)

Prep time: 25 min

Chef Kevin

72 BRINE FOR MEATS

Ingredients

1 gallon H2O

1 cup Kosher salt—must be
   Diamon Crystal Red Box,

otherwise you will have to adjust
ratio

Instructions

Marinate overnight.

Yield: 10 people
Prep time: 10 min

Chef Kevin

73   STUFFED BELL PEPPERS

Ingredients

12 cups Marinara sauce

6 cups Beef broth

6 tbsp Balsamic vinegar

1 ½ tsp Crushed red pepper flakes

3 Red onions

3 Yellow onions

6 tbsp Olive oil—sauté onions

Divide in half. Place half of the sautéed onions in the sauce and the other half in the meat mixture.

6 lbs Ground beef

1 ½ lbs Raw sausage

60 oz Diced tomatoes

1 ½ cups Fresh parsley chopped

8 tbsp Chopped garlic

12 tsp Kosher salt

6 tsp Black pepper

½ tsp Cayenne

6 cups Grated Parmesan cheese

6 cups Jasmine rice—9 cups
    H_2O—cook

Instructions

1. Line pans with marinara.
2. Stuff ½ peppers with mixture.
3. 375 oven, 45 min covered.
4. Top with grated Parmesan cheese. Bake uncovered to 160 center.

Yield: 50 people

Prep time: 90 min

Chef Kevin

74   AHI TUNA SUSHI ROLLS

Ingredients

3 cups Jasmine rice   4 ½ cups H2O—cook/cool

Sprinkle with rice vinegar.

3 lbs Raw ¼ inch diced ahi tuna—   1 cup Mayo
   some/all rough chop in robo   2 tsp Kosher salt
   coup   1 tsp Black pepper
1 bunch Green onions sliced   Seaweed papers
½ Cucumber seeded ¼ inch diced   Soy sauce
1 Avocado   Wasabi soy sauce
2 tbsp Siracha   Pickled ginger

Yield: 40 people
Prep time: 90 min

Chef Kevin

75   KEVIN'S CHICKEN WINGS

Ingredients
Approx. 50 each large jumbo wings

Brine overnight

Instructions
1. Pan spray and season both sides:

Kosher salt	Thyme
Black pepper	Paprika
Granulated garlic	

2. Oven temp 300.
3. Cook time Approx. 1 hour.
4. Center temp goal 185.
5. Cool, reheat to 140.
6. Frank's RedHot/BBQ sauce.
7. Blue cheese, celery sticks.

Yield: 30–40 people (appetizer)
Prep time: 20 min

Chef Kevin

76   KING FISHER WARM CRAB DIP

Ingredients

1 lb Cream cheese

1 lb Sour cream

Mix above together.

1 tsp Onion powder
1 tbsp Garlic powder
1 tbsp Kosher salt
3 tbsp Cajun seasoning
⅛ cup Dijon mustard

3 tbsp Roast garlic
¾ qt Shredded cheddar cheese
¾ qt Shredded fontina cheese
2 cups Green onions sliced

Instructions

1. Mix above together.
2. Fold in crab last.
3. About 1 ½–2 lb.
4. Heat slowly to 140.
5. Serve with bread/chips.

Yield: 40+ people
Prep time: 45 min

Chef Kevin

77   COLESLAW DRESSING

Ingredients

5 cups Mayo

1 cup Olive oil

2 tbsp Kosher salt

1 tbsp Black pepper

1 cup Chopped garlic

1 cup Red wine vinegar

2 tbsp Sambal oelek

1 bunch Cilantro

1 cup Lime juice

Mix together.

Green cabbage

Red cabbage

Red onion

Bell peppers

Cucumbers

Shred carrots

Green onions

Yield: 50 people

Prep time: 60 min

Chef Kevin

78   TROPICAL BBQ SALSA

Ingredients

½ cup Olive oil

1 Red onion ¼ inch diced

1 tbsp Kosher salt

1 tbsp Black pepper

3 cups Pineapple ¼ inch diced

2 cups Chopped mango cubes

1 cup Apple cider vinegar

1 tsp Red pepper flakes

Instructions

1. Sauté and blend to slightly chunky.
2. Add 3 40 oz bottles of your favorite BBQ sauce.

Yield: 50 people

Prep time: 30 min

Chef Kevin

79   HORSERADISH CREAM SAUCE

Ingredients

5 tbsp Horseradish fresh
1 cup Mayo
1 cup Sour cream
1 tbsp Kosher salt

1 tbsp Black pepper
5 tbsp Chopped garlic
½ cup Olive oil

Instructions

Mix above together.

Yield: 20 people
Prep time: 15 min

Chef Kevin

80   SMOKED SALMON CHOWDER

Ingredients

3 qt Potatoes ½ inch diced, cooked in salt H2O about 8–9 min al dente

½ lb Bacon ¼ inch diced

3 tbsp Olive oil

¾ qt Yellow onion ½ inch diced

2 tbsp Chopped garlic

¼ qt Carrots ½ inch diced

1 qt Celery ¼ inch diced

1 tbsp Kosher salt

2 tbsp Smoked paprika

1 cup White wine reduced ½

¾ lb Butter

1 lb Flour

2 46 oz can Clams—separate juice

1 46 oz Chicken stock

3 46 oz Clam juice only—make from base

Preheat liquid to 150 separately.

2 tbsp Kosher salt

1 can Tomato paste

Last, add clams and potatoes.

1 ½ lbs Smoked/fresh salmon

¾ qt Heavy cream

Yield: 4 gallons
Prep time: 1 hour

Chef Kevin

81   DEVILED EGGS

Put enough H2O in pan to just cover 1 layer of eggs 20–24 each. Bring H2O to a boil—gently lower in eggs. Cook 11 min—then cool, peel, cut in half, remove yolk.

To yolk add:

1 tbsp Chopped garlic   1 tsp Black pepper
1 tbsp Dijon mustard   2 Queen olives ⅛ inch diced
5 tbsp Blue cheese dressing   ¼ tsp Tabasco
1 tsp Kosher salt

Instructions
1. Mix above together.
2. Stuff eggs, sprinkle with paprika.

Yield: 40 people
Prep time: 45 min

Chef Kevin

82   MINESTRONE SOUP

Ingredients

1 Yellow onion ¼ inch diced
1 Carrot ¼ inch diced
3 stalks Celery ¼ inch diced
4 tbsp Olive oil
2 cups Broccoli ½ inch diced
¼ of White cabbage ½ inch diced
1 can Kidney beans

1 can Garbanzo beans
1 Zucchini ¼ inch diced
1 Yellow squash ¼ inch diced
2 Red potatoes ½ inch diced
2 Tomatoes ½ inch diced
1 cup White wine ½ reduced
3 qt Chicken base

Instructions

1. Slurry to thicken.
2. Add pasta at service time.

Yield: 2 gallons (25 people)
Prep time: 35 min

Chef Kevin

83   PEANUT BUTTER COOKIES

Ingredients

½ cup Butter softened
½ cup Peanut butter
½ cup Sugar
½ cup Brown sugar
1 Egg
1 ¼ cups Flour

¾ tsp Bake soda
½ tsp Bake powder
½ tsp Kosher salt
½ cup Chocolate chips
½ cup Oatmeal

Instructions

1. Mix dry/wet separately.
2. Meatball-size scoop.
3. Press with fork crisscross.
4. 350 for 12–13 min.

Yield: 20 people
Prep time: 30 min

Chef Kevin

84   DRY BEAN HUMMUS

Ingredients
1 lb Dry garbanzo beans   ¼ cup Kosher salt
1 gallon H2O

Instructions
1. Bring to boil.
2. Simmer beans about ½ hour al dente.
3. Cool beans.

Robo coup:

Beans
1 tbsp Kosher salt   2 Lemons juiced
1 tbsp Sesame oil   2 cups Olive oil

Add the olive oil slowly.

Yield: 20 people
Prep time: 30 min

Chef Kevin

85   CREAMED SPINACH

Ingredients

30 oz Chopped spinach, frozen

2 tbsp Butter

1 Yellow onion ¼ inch diced

6 cloves Garlic sliced

4 oz Cream cheese

1 cup Heavy cream

1 cup Shredded mozzarella

½ cup Grated Parmesan cheese

Kosher salt

Black pepper

Yield: 10 people

Prep time: 30 min

Chef Kevin

86   COFFEE CAKE

1 stick Soft butter	¾ cup Sugar

Cream above in mixer.

1 tsp Vanilla	1 Egg

Add above to mixer.

2 cups Flour	¼ tsp Kosher salt
2 tsp Bake powder	

Mix above. Put half in mixer with milk.

¾ cup Milk	2 tbsp Instant expresso

Mix above.

After batter mixes together, add second half of flour.

5 tbsp Butter soft	½ cup Brown sugar
¾ cup Flour	1 tbsp Cinnamon

Mix above.

3 tbsp Butter soft	1 tsp Cinnamon
½ cup Flour	½ cup Brown sugar

Mix above.

Put half batter in 9x9 pan. Put center mix in, then other half batter on top. 350 for 40–45 min—toothpick clean.

Yield: 10 people
Prep time: 45 min

Chef Kevin

87   COLLARD GREENS

Ingredients

1 tbsp Olive oil

3 slices Bacon 1 inch diced

1 Yellow onion ¼ inch diced

2 tbsp Chopped garlic

Instructions

1. Cook bacon, remove.
2. Cook onion and garlic in bacon fat.

1 lb Collard greens—cook down

3 cups Chicken broth

1 tsp Kosher salt

1 tsp Black pepper

½ tsp Red pepper flakes

3. Simmer 45–60 min to tender.

    Yield: 10 people

    Prep time: 30 min

    Chef Kevin

88   SOUS VIDE BRISKET

Ingredients

1 piece of Brisket cut to fit in
   gallon bags
Liquid smoke

Beef broth
Kosher salt
Black pepper

Instructions

137 for 3 days

Yield: 8 oz per person portion
Prep time: 20 min

Chef Kevin

89   TIRAMISU

Ingredients

4 cups Black coffee	8x18 glass pan
2 oz Kahlúa	8 Egg yolks
2 tbsp Instant expresso	½ cup Sugar

Instructions

1. Beat until peaks form.

1 ½ cups Heavy cream	1 oz Kahlúa
½ cup Sugar	2 tbsp Expresso
2 cups Mascarpone cheese	

2. Dip ladyfingers in coffee quickly—like 1 ½ seconds.
3. Line pan with cocoa powdered sugar mix shaker. Place one layer of coffee-dipped ladyfingers in pan—top with cream, then the eggs and sugar, then another layer of ladyfingers, then top with cream.

Yield: 10–15 people
Prep time: 45 min

Chef Kevin

90   CLASSIC STEAK TARTARE

Ingredients

3 tbsp Olive oil

2 tbsp Whole grain mustard

1 tbsp Red wine vinegar

1 tbsp Capers chopped

1 tsp Dijon mustard

Sprinkle of cayenne

1 tsp Sambal oelek

1 lb Chopped cold fresh beef ¼ inch diced—I use filet mignon

1 Shallot or sub red onion finely diced

1 Egg yolk

2 tbsp Fresh parsley

Kosher salt

Instructions

1. Mix above together.
2. Top/garnish with whole egg yolk.
3. Serve with toasted bread and/or potato chips.

Yield: 20 people

Prep time: 30 min

Chef Kevin

91   PALM BEACH CHEESE PUFFS

Ingredients

1 loaf White bread   4 tbsp Melted butter
Circle cutter—1 ½ inch round   ¼ tsp Granulated garlic

Instructions

1. Mix above together.
2. Paint butter on one side of the bread circle.
3. Toast butter side up.
4. 375 at 15 min—cool.

¾ cup Mayo   1 tbsp Sweet onion 1/16 inch diced
½ cup Grated Parmesan

5. Put above mixture on bread.
6. Cook just before service.
7. 375 oven for 15 min golden brown.

Yield: 10 people
Prep time: 45 min

Chef Kevin

92   GERMAN POTATO SALAD

Ingredients

3 lbs Red potato ¼ inch sliced
Cook in salt H2O until al dente.

1 lb Bacon 1 inch diced
Cook in 4 tbsp olive oil.

Remove bacon from pan.

1 Red onion ¼ inch diced
½ cup Apple cider vinegar
3 tbsp Sugar
1 ½ tbsp Dijon mustard
¾ tsp Kosher salt

½ tsp Black pepper
1 ½ tbsp Chopped garlic
¾ cup Fresh chopped parsley or 2
   tbsp dry
Chives as garnish ⅛ inch slices

Yield: 20 people
Prep time: 45 min

Chef Kevin

93   ALABAMA WHITE BBQ SAUCE

Ingredients

2 cups Mayo

½ cup Apple cider vinegar

2 tbsp Lemon juice

1 tbsp Worcestershire sauce

2 tsp Ground black pepper

1 tsp Kosher salt

1 tsp Cayenne

2 tsp Horseradish

1 tsp Chopped garlic

Yield: 3 cups (10–15 people)

Prep time: 15 min

Chef Kevin

94   APPLE CIDER VINAIGRETTE

Ingredients

1 cup Apple cider vinegar

1 ½ cups Olive oil

2 tbsp Kosher salt

1 tbsp Black pepper

2 tbsp Dijon mustard

1 tbsp Grain mustard

Instructions

1. Blend in blender.
2. Add oil slowly.

Yield: 2 cups (10 people)

Prep time: 10 min

Chef Kevin

95   EATON MESS DESSERT

Ingredients

6 Egg whites   ¼ tsp Cream of tarter
1 tsp Vanilla   1 ½ cups Sugar

Instructions

1. Whip until peaks form.
2. Piping bag—star tip.
3. Place golf ball-size stars on parchment paper and sheet tray.
4. 200 oven at 2 hours-plus.
5. Serve with blueberry sauce.
6. Whipped cream, blueberries.

Standard whipped cream
2 cups Heavy cream   ½ cup Powdered sugar
1 tsp Vanilla

Yield: 10–15 people
Prep time: 45 min

Chef Kevin

96   CLUB CAR CHICKEN MARINADE

Ingredients

8 oz Red onion

4 tbsp Chopped garlic

1 oz Fresh jalapeño

½ oz Fresh parsley

½ oz Italian parsley

½ oz Fresh basil or 1 tbsp dry

1 tsp Granulated onion

1 tsp Granulated garlic

1 tsp Paprika

1 tbsp Oregano

1 tbsp Black pepper

1 cup Red wine vinegar

3 tbsp Kosher salt

1 tbsp Celery salt

4 Lemons juiced

3 tbsp Garlic salt

6 cups Olive oil

Instructions

1. Blend above ingredients together in blender.
2. Add oil slowly.
3. Marinate chicken overnight.

Yield: 50 people

Prep time: 30 min

Chef Kevin

97   COD FISH WITH LENTILS

Ingredients

1 cup Flat leaf parsley   ⅓ cup Capers
1 cup Basil   ½ cup Gherkins chopped
1 cup Mint   2 tbsp Dijon mustard

Instructions

1. Robo coup above.
2. Add olive oil to make a paste.
3. Cook lentils in plain H2O about 20 min—al dente.

Kosher salt   Cod fish—pan sear to done
Black pepper

Topping:
Olive oil
Fresh garlic sliced   Kosher salt
Lemon juice   Black pepper

Yield: 8 oz fish per person
Prep time: 45 min

Chef Kevin

98   WARM BACON SOY DRESSING

Ingredients

1 lb Bacon ¼ inch diced—save oil
¼ Red onion ¼ inch diced
1 cup Apple cider vinegar
¼ cup Dijon mustard
¼ cup Sugar

1 tsp Kosher salt
1 tsp Black pepper
¼ cup Soy sauce
1 Fresh jalapeño ⅛ inch diced

Instructions

1. Blend all ingredients in blender except bacon—serve warm.
2. Salad—seared ahi tuna, goat cheese, avocado.

Yield: 10+
Prep time: 30 min

Chef Kevin

99   BRAISED PORK BELLY

Score pork belly ¼ inch crisscross.
Kosher salt skin side—sear 4 min.
Remove meat.

1 cup Olive oil in very hot pan
Sauté veggies in pan:

1 yellow onion 1 inch chopped   1 bunch Celery 1 inch chopped
4 Carrots 1 inch chopped

Resalt fat side skin up, add fennel seeds.

1 tbsp Kosher salt   10 Bay leaves
1 tbsp Black pepper   2 Fennel bulbs 1 inch cubes

Deglaze with 2 cups white wine.

1 tbsp Fennel seed in pan   2 qt H2O
4 tbsp Chopped garlic   2 tbsp Chicken base

Bring stock just up to skin level—not over. Bring to a boil on stovetop.
Transfer to oven—2 ½ hours.
Cool, portion.
Slider buns—mayo chimichurri mix.

Yield: 40 people
Prep time: 40 min

Chef Kevin

100   ASIAN DRESSING #3

Ingredients

¾ cup Olive oil   3 tbsp Honey
½ cup Soy sauce   3 tsp Chopped garlic
⅓ cup Rice vinegar   2 tbsp Fresh grated ginger
¼ cup H2O

Instructions

Blend above in blender.

Yield: 10 people
Prep time: 20 min

Chef Kevin

101   TRAEGER FILET MIGNON #1

Pull beef tenderloin out at noon.

Season:

Kosher salt	Paprika
Black pepper	Thyme
Granulated garlic	Montreal steak seasoning
Celery salt	

3:00 p.m.	Turn grill on	205
3:30	Meat on grill	50
4:00	Flip	80
4:30	Flip	100
5:00	Flip	110
5:30	Flip	120
6:00	Flip	125
6:30	Flip/turn off grill	130

Yield: 1 tenderloin = 7–8 people
Prep time: 60 min for 50 people

Chef Kevin

102   MAC AND CHEESE #2

Ingredients

5 gallon pot ¾ full H2O

1 ½ cups Kosher salt

5 lbs Pasta elbows

7 min cook time—cool pasta.

½ lb Butter

3 tbsp Olive oil

1 tsp Saffron

½ lb Flour

4 tbsp Kosher salt

1 tbsp Black pepper

2 tbsp Chicken base

2 qt Half and half

5 cups Heavy cream

4 oz Shredded Parmesan cheese

4 oz Grated Parmesan cheese

1 tsp Hot pepper flakes

4 oz Diced American cheese

4 oz Diced pepper jack cheese

2 lbs Shredded fontina cheese

Instructions

1. In sauce pan, bring the above ingredients together until melted.
2. Add melted ingredients to cooled pasta.
3. Place combined ingredients in sprayed baking pan.
4. Bake to center temperature of 140.

Yield: 50 people

Prep time: 60 min

Chef Kevin

103   MANHATTAN CLAM CHOWDER

Ingredients

4 tbsp Olive oil
2 Onions ¼ inch diced
4 stalks Celery ¼ inch diced
¼ tsp Red pepper flakes
½ cup Tomato paste

½ cup Fresh chopped parsley or 1 tbsp dry
1 tsp Thyme
2 Bay leaves
4 Potatoes ½ inch diced; precook 7–9 min al dente

10 cups Clam/tomato base mix
56 oz Canned tomato product
3 cups Clams or conch

2 tbsp Kosher salt
1 tbsp Black pepper
Cornstarch slurry to thicken

Yield: 1 ½ gallon (20 people)
Prep time: 50 min

Chef Kevin

104   PUDDING LAYER DESSERT

Ingredients

1 cup Pecans chopped   ½ cup Melted butter
3 tbsp Sugar   1 cup Flour

Instructions

1. Mix above together.
2. Press into a bake pan.
3. Bake 20 min.
4. Mix 8 oz cream cheese.
5. Room temp.

1 cup Powdered sugar   2 cups Milk
1 cup Cool Whip (or homemade   5.1 oz Chocolate pudding
   whipped cream)   2 cups Milk
5.1 oz Instant vanilla pudding 2 cups Cool Whip topping

Yield: 20 people
Prep time: 45 min

Chef Kevin

105   TRAEGER PRIME RIB

Pull prime ribs out of walk-in at about 10 a.m. Start to bring to room temp.

Clean prime ribs.

Season:

Kosher salt	Paprika
Black pepper	Celery salt
Granulated garlic	Montreal steak seasoning
Thyme	

1:30 p.m.	Turn smoker on	200
2:00	Meat on gill	43
2:30	Flip	50
3:00	Flip	60
3:30	Flip	70
4:00	Flip	80
4:30	Flip	90
5:00	Flip	100
5:30	Flip	110
6:00	Flip	120
6:30	Flip	125
6:30	Turn smoker off.	
6:45	Remove/rest meat.	

Yield: 1 prime rib (15 people)
Prep time: 15 min per

Chef Kevin

106   **CAJUN CARROTS**

Ingredients

1 Large carrot per person
Cut carrots bias ¼ inch.
2 cups Olive oil
¼ cup Kosher salt
⅛ cup Black pepper

¼ cup Smoked paprika
¼ cup Granulated garlic
¼ cup Thyme
¼ cup Cajun seasoning

Instructions

1. 350 about 30 min to fork tender.
2. Reheat BEFORE service.

Yield: 50 people
Prep time: 45 min

Chef Kevin

107   CONCH CHOWDER

Ingredients

2 tbsp Olive oil

8 oz Bacon ¼ inch diced

½ cup Flour

Remove from pan.

2 tbsp Olive oil

1 tbsp Kosher salt

1 tbsp Black pepper

2 Yellow onions ¼ inch diced

4 stalks Celery ¼ inch diced

2 Carrots ¼ inch diced

1 Green bell pepper

1 Fresh jalapeño ⅛ inch diced

8 Small waxy potatoes

1 cup Tomato puree

6 cups Clam base stock juice

1 can Conch—separate juice

½ tsp Red pepper flakes

½ tsp Tabasco

Instructions

Put conch in soup just BEFORE serving.

Yield: 1 ½ gallons (20 people)

Prep time: 45 min

Chef Kevin

108   CLUB CAR CLAM CHOWDER

Ingredients

8 lbs Peeled potatoes ½ inch diced
Use 5 gallon pot ¾ full H2O.
1 ½ cups Kosher salt
Cook al dente 8 min avg. Cool. Set aside.
3 cans Clams (46 oz each)—separate juice
Make 4 cans of clam juice from clam base.
Heat all juice separate to 150.

4 tbsp Olive oil	2 tbsp Thyme
1 lb Bacon ¼ inch diced	2 tbsp Chopped garlic
38 oz Celery ¼ inch diced	2 cups White wine—reduced by ½
27 oz Onions ¼ inch diced	1 ¼ lbs Butter
2 tbsp Kosher salt	21 oz Flour—make roux

Instructions

1. Add roux to pan with juice.
2. Simmer to thick.
3. Add 1 ½ qt heavy cream.
4. Add potatoes and clams last so they don't overcook.

Yield: 4 gallons
Prep time: 60 min

Chef Kevin

109   GREEN BEAN CASSEROLE

Ingredients

4 cans Condensed mushroom soup   24 cans Green beans
Squeeze and remove all juice.

2 Yellow onions ⅛ inch Julianne   2 tbsp Black pepper
1 tbsp Chicken base   2 cups Feta cheese
½ cup Olive oil   3 cups Jack cheddar shredded
3 tbsp Chopped garlic   3 ½ cups Fontina shredded
2 tbsp Kosher salt

Instructions

1. Mix above together.
2. Put in pan, cover with foil.
3. 350 bake about 1 hour.
4. 140 center temp.
5. Add crushed potato chips on top.

Yield: 40 people
Prep time: 50 min

Chef Kevin

110   PINEAPPLE BAKED BEANS

Ingredients

7 cans (28 oz) Bush's baked beans
2 Yellow onions ½ inch diced
½ cup Olive oil
5 tbsp Chopped garlic

1 cup Yellow mustard
3 cups BBQ sauce
1 Pineapple ½ inch diced

Instructions

Simmer on low heat.

Yield: 40 people
Prep time: 25 min

Chef Kevin

111   VEGAN BUTTERNUT SQUASH QUESO

Ingredients

2 cups Peeled and diced Yukon gold potatoes

1 cup Peeled and diced butternut squash

Cook above separately until tender.

Place the hot cooked potatoes and squash into the blender.

½ cup Yellow onion ¼ inch diced—sauté

½ cup Cashews raw

¼ cup Olive oil

¼ + 2 tbsp Hot H2O

¼ cup Fresh lemon juice

2 tbsp Apple cider vinegar

2 cloves or 2 tsp Chopped garlic

1 tsp Smoked paprika

½ tsp Cayenne

1 tsp Kosher salt

Blend all together.

Topping:

1 Avocado ½ inch diced

½ of Lime juiced

½ tsp Kosher salt

¼ cup Black beans

¼ cup Diced tomato

2 tbsp Onion ¼ inch diced

1 Jalapeño ¼ inch diced

¼ cup Cilantro

Yield: 10 people
Prep time: 45 min

Chef Kevin

112 GARBANZO HARISSA VEGAN BURGER

Ingredients

1 tbsp Ground flax seed
3 tbsp H2O
1 tbsp Olive oil
1 cup Yellow onion ¼ inch diced
½ tsp Kosher salt
1 cup Chopped walnuts
2 tsp Ground cumin
2 tsp Smoked paprika

½ tsp Black pepper
3 cloves or 2 tsp Minced garlic
¼ cup Harissa
1 ½ cups Chickpeas
1 cup Cooked warm, sticky short-grain brown rice
2 tbsp Fresh lemon juice
⅓ cup Panko

Instructions

1. Mix above together.
2. Form burger patties.
3. Sear both sides, finish in oven.
4. 160–180 center temp.

Yield: 6 people
Prep time: 30 min

Chef Kevin

113   TRAEGER FILET MIGNON #2

Pull beef to start to get toward room temp around noon.

3:30 p.m.—Turn grill to 205.

Meat temp at 3:30 is 50.

Season with:

Kosher salt	Paprika
Black pepper	Thyme
Granulated garlic	Montreal steak seasoning
Celery salt	

4:00 p.m.	Meat on grill	
4:30	Flip	80
5:00	Flip	100
5:30	Flip	110
6:00	Flip	120
6:30	Flip	125, turn to 165
7:00	Flip	Turn grill off
7:15	Bring inside	127–128

Yield: 1 filet = 7–8 people

Prep time: 60 min

Chef Kevin

114   RED WINE DEMI

Ingredients

2 cups Red wine   3 Bay leaves
⅓ of Yellow onion ½ inch diced   1 tsp Thyme
5 cloves Whole garlic cut in half

Instructions

1. Reduce to about ½ cup liquid.
2. Strain liquid.
3. Add meat juices from sous vide meats, or make a beef broth from a base—about 1 quart.
4. Bring to a boil, reduce a bit. Slurry to thicken. Season as needed with salt.
5. Butter BEFORE service.
6. Heavy cream—if desired.

Yield: 10 people
Prep time: 30 min

Chef Kevin

115   TRAEGER SMOKED SALMON

Remove salmon from marinade.

Put on a sheet tray that is lined with foil. Place a metal grate on foil for air circulation.

8:50 a.m.	Turn smoker to 165.
9:20 a.m.	Put salmon on.
9:50 a.m.	85
10:30 a.m.	95
11:15 a.m.	Done—center temp 110.

Smoked salmon takes about 2 hours.

I've also done it at 180.

Yield: 1 filet = 10 people (appetizer)

Prep time: 30 min

Chef Kevin

116   BLACK BEAN BURGERS

Ingredients

2 15 oz cans Black beans drained and rinsed

4 oz Chopped ¼ inch diced yellow onion

1 tbsp Chopped garlic

1 Egg

2 Green onions sliced

1 cup Panko

½ cup Feta cheese

1 Chipotle pepper ⅛ inch diced

1 tbsp Balsamic vinegar

2 tsp Cumin

1 tsp Kosher salt

1 tsp Black pepper

½ tsp Red pepper flakes

Instructions

1. Form into patties.
2. Season both sides with Kosher salt and pepper. Sear.
3. Finish in oven to 160.

Yield: about 8 burgers
Prep time: 30 min

Chef Kevin

117   HOMEMADE PORK BELLY BACON

Cut pork belly into slabs that can fit into 1 gallon bags.

¾ cup H2O   4 ½ tsp Black pepper
6 tbsp Dark brown sugar   ½ tsp Prague powder
4 ½ tsp Kosher salt

4 days marinade.
Turn over once per day.
Smoker 225 2 hours until temp hits 150.

Yield: 1 whole loin (20 people)
Prep time: 30 min

Chef Kevin

118   TROPICAL SALSA BASE

Ingredients

2 cups Fresh pineapple ¼ inch diced

2 cups Fresh or jar mango ¼ inch diced

Juice of 3 Limes

½ Cucumber seeded ¼ inch diced

1 ½ tsp Kosher salt

1 tsp Black pepper

3 tbsp Olive oil

1 Red bell pepper ¼ inch diced

3 tbsp Chopped garlic

¼ of Red onion ⅛ inch diced

3 Green onions ⅛ inch sliced

Instructions

1. Combine all above.
2. Adjust seasoning (salt) just BEFORE service.

Yield: 20 people

Prep time: 30 min

Chef Kevin

119   SEAFOOD CAKES

Ingredients

2 ½ lbs Seafood—crab, black cod, shrimp

2 tbsp Chopped garlic

2 Whole eggs

2 Egg whites

¼ cup Worcestershire sauce

1 tsp Cayenne

1 tbsp Kosher salt

1 cup Panko

1 cup Italian breadcrumbs

1 tsp Cajun seasoning

1 cup Shredded mozzarella

Instructions

1. Mix together.
2. Meatball-size scoop.
3. Sear both sides.
4. Finish in oven if needed.
5. Center temp 150–160.

Yield: 40 people

Prep time: 45 min

Chef Kevin

120   GERMAN CHOCOLATE CAKE

Frosting:

1 can Sweetened condensed milk   1 tsp Vanilla
3 Eggs, yolk slightly beaten   1 ⅓ cups Coconut flakes
½ cup Butter softened   1 cup Chopped pecans

In saucepan combine condensed milk, egg yolks, and butter.
Stir frequently to 180.
Then add vanilla, coconut, and nuts. Cool to room temp.

2 cups Heavy cream   2 ¼ cups Sugar
¼ cup Cocoa powder   1 tsp Vanilla extract
½ cup Powdered sugar   4 Eggs
1 cup Mascarpone   2 cups Flour
¼ cup Cocoa   1 tsp Bake soda
½ cup Hot H2O   1 tsp Kosher salt
1 cup + 3 tbsp Butter softened   1 cup Buttermilk

Oven 350. Grease and parchment 3 9-inch round pans.
Stir cocoa and H2O—set aside.
Beat butter, sugar, and vanilla.
Add eggs one at a time.
Combine flour, bake soda, salt.
Mix. Alternate each mixture to blender till done. Pour batter into 3 pans.
About 20 min—toothpick.

Yield: 12–18 pieces (20 people)
Prep time: 1 ½ hours

Chef Kevin

121   COLD SMOKED SALMON

Ingredients

5 filets Salmon deboned

5 cups White sugar

5 cups Brown sugar

5 tbsp Dill

5 tbsp Fennel

2 ½ cups Kosher salt

Instructions

1. Make recipe x2.
2. Cover salmon top and bottom side.
3. Cover. Refrigerate 36 hours.

Yield: 1 filet = 10 people (appetizer)

Prep time: 30 min

Chef Kevin

122   RIBOLLITA SOUP

Ingredients

8 tbsp Olive oil

2 Red onions ½ inch diced

6 stalks Celery ½ inch diced

6 Carrots ¼ inch diced

4 tbsp Kosher salt

2 tbsp Black pepper

12 cloves Garlic sliced

56 oz Canned diced tomatoes

2 cups Dry white wine

Reduce ½.

8 cups Vegetable broth

30 oz Cannellini beans

Place one more can of the beans in blender with 1 cup of soup broth—this will help thicken the soup. Blend, then return to soup.

2 inches Parmesan rind cheese

1 tbsp Thyme

2 Bay leaves

2 tsp Oregano

1 tsp Crushed red pepper flakes

2 lbs Kale or spinach

Serve with sourdough bread.

Yield: 2 gallons (20+ people)

Prep time: 40 min

Chef Kevin

123   DINNER ROLLS

Ingredients

3 cups Flour

2 tbsp Rapid rise yeast

⅓ cup Sugar

1 tsp Kosher salt

1 ½ cups 109 or less whole milk

5 tbsp Melted butter

1 Egg

Instructions

1. Mix above with dough hook.
2. Add up to 2 more cups flour until a ball of dough forms.
3. Scrape sides as needed on low speed—then beat on medium speed for 3 min or so.
4. Put in oiled bowl—rise 30 min.
5. Form into golf ball size.
6. Put in bake pan—rise 30 min.
7. Bake 375 for 15 min. Paint tops with melted butter.
8. Sprinkle with sea salt.

Yield: 20 people

Prep time: 45 min

Chef Kevin

124   BLUEBERRY POUND CAKE

2 13x9 glass pans = 32 people
Sarah Lee pound cake 1 lb each, 3 total
Line bottom of pans with pound cake, about ⅓ inch thick. Splash blueberry
sauce on each piece of pound cake.

Blueberry Syrup
1 lb Blueberries   16 oz H_2O
16 oz sugar   1 tbsp Vanilla

Heat, cool, strain.

Whipped Cream
1 lb Mascarpone cheese   ½ cup Blueberry syrup
2 pints Heavy cream   1 ½ cups Powdered sugar

Add 1 lb fresh blueberries to finished whipped cream.
Line pan on top of pound cake.
Place ½ inch of the whipped cream mix on top of the pound cake layer in the pan.
Add remaining 2 pints heavy cream to remaining leftover whipped cream.
Add:
1 ½ cup Powdered sugar   1 tbsp Vanilla
Add another layer of pound cake.
Splash with blueberry sauce.
Top with remaining whipped cream.
Sprinkle with fresh blueberries.

Yield: 40 people
Prep time: 45 min

Chef Kevin

125   RICE KRISPIES TREATS

Ingredients

3 tbsp Butter   6 cups Rice Krispies cereal

5 ½ cups Mini marshmallows

Instructions

1. Melt butter on low heat.
2. Add marshmallows. Stir together until melted.
3. Remove from heat.
4. Add cereal. Mix together.
5. Put in a greased pan.
6. Cool. Remove, cut, serve.

Yield: 10 people

Prep time: 30 min

Chef Kevin

126   ITALIAN WEDDING SOUP

Ingredients

2 tbsp Kosher salt
1 tbsp Black pepper
4 Yellow onions ½ inch diced
5 cups Carrots ¼ inch diced
8 stalks Celery
½ cup Whole cloves garlic crushed
32 cups Vegetable/chicken/tomato
    broth combo
8 tsp Italian seasoning

3 cups Israel couscous—precook
    5 min
2 lbs Fresh/frozen kale, spinach,
    or a combination of both equal
    to this weight
1 tbsp Kosher salt
1 tbsp Black pepper
2 cups White wine—reduce by ½

Instructions

1. Meatball recipe.
2. Appetizer size—nickel.

Yield: about 3 gallons
Prep time: 45 min

Chef Kevin

127   OYSTER STUFFING

4 tbsp Olive oil
½ of Yellow onion ¼ inch diced
2 stalks Celery ¼ inch diced

½ Jalapeño ⅛ inch diced
2 tsp Kosher salt
1 tsp Black pepper

Sauté above to tender.

¾ stick (6 tbsp) Butter
1 ½ cups liquid total—use liquid from oyster jar, then H2O to make 1 ½ cups.

Bring to boil.

Add 1 box Chicken stovetop box stuffing
Remove from heat—put ½ amount of stuffing in 8x8 bake pan.
Put drained, paper towel-dried oysters on stuffing—cold. Top with other
½ of stuffing.
Bake 350 about 15–20 min to 140.

Yield: 10 people
Prep time: 45 min

Chef Kevin

128   DUTCH OVEN WHITE BREAD

Ingredients
3 cups All-purpose flour   ½ tsp Instant yeast
1 ½ tsp Kosher salt

Instructions
1. Mix above dry ingredients together.
2. Add 1 ½ cups room temp H2O.
3. Mix with a spatula, then cover in bowl. Let sit 6–12 hours.
4. Preheat oven 450.
5. Preheat Dutch oven for ½ hour.
6. Flour on cutting board.
7. Scrape bowl bread onto cutting board—knead into a formed ball, adding flour as needed.
8. Place on parchment paper inside Dutch oven.
9. Cook 30 min with lid on.
10. Cook 8–10 min with lid off.

Yield: 10 people
Prep time: 15 min

Chef Kevin

129   CRAB REMICK

Ingredients

1 ½ cups Mayo

½ cup Chili sauce (Mae Ploy)

2 tsp Dijon mustard

1 tbsp Tabasco sauce

3 tbsp Tarragon vinegar or sub
white vinegar

3 tbsp Worcestershire sauce

2 tsp Celery salt

¼ cup Fresh tarragon chopped or
1 ½ tbsp dry tarragon

2 tsp Garlic minced

½ bunch Green onions sliced

1 lb Jumbo lump crabmeat or use
real crabmeat from legs—snow
king, etc.—or buy a good
canned meat

5 strips Bacon, slight crispy—cut
in 1 inch strips

Instructions

1. Serve with rice.
2. Broil Parmesan cheese grated on top.
3. 400—15 min to 140.

Yield: 10 people

Prep time: 30 min

Chef Kevin

130   SHRIMP BURGER

Ingredients

1 ½ lbs Raw shrimp

½ cup Yellow onion ¼ inch diced

½ cup Celery ¼ inch diced

¼ cup Red bell pepper ¼ inch diced

2 Large eggs beaten

½ tsp Cajun

½ tsp Old Bay

1 tsp Kosher salt

¼ tsp Cayenne

¼ cup Green onions

¼ cup Chopped parsley

1 tsp Bake powder

½ cup Mayo

1 sleeve Saltine crackers crumbled

Instructions

1. Form into meatball-size balls—flatten for slider—on Hawaii bun.
2. Try cooking as meatballs—serve with pasta with butter garlic sauce.

Yield: 10 people

Prep time: 45 min

Chef Kevin

131   RED WINE PEARS DESSERT

Ingredients

10 Bosc pears (peel off skin)   4 cups Red Wine
1 cup Sugar   1 cup OJ
2 Large oranges—peels   4 tsp Vanilla extract
16 Whole cloves   4 oz Dry cherries
2 sticks Cinnamon   4 oz Dry plumbs

Instructions

1. Place peeled pears in liquid and bring to a simmer.
2. Poach/simmer about 30 min.
3. Let cool in liquid.
4. Serve with chocolate sauce and boiled-down/thickened red wine sauce liquid above.

Yield: 10 people
Prep time: 45 min

Chef Kevin

132   CHEF KEVIN'S BREAD PUDDING

Deep dish pan—12x18 or approx.
Spray pan.

Ingredients

1 can Condensed milk

2 pieces New York cheesecake

1 cup Sugar

1 tbsp Vanilla

5 Eggs

1 tbsp Kosher salt

2 tsp Cinnamon

4 cups Heavy cream

3 packs Raisins (3 oz)

2 sticks Butter—sliced ¼ inch thin

1 layer Sara Lee Artisan White Bread

1 layer Cinnamon raisin bread

Instructions

1. Sub any bread for the above.
2. Soak bread for about 1 min.
3. Start to layer in pan.
4. Put butter pieces on bread.
5. Build to 3 layers.
6. Sprinkle in remaining batter.
7. Bake 375 for about 1 hour.

Yield: 10–15 people
Prep time: 45 min

Chef Kevin

133   BOURBON SAUCE

Ingredients

1 cup Butter soft
2 cups Sugar
2 Large eggs beaten well

1 tsp Vanilla
4 tbsp Bourbon

Instructions

1. Heat butter and sugar until dissolved.
2. Add eggs; stir and heat to 175. Eggs set at 175.
3. Remove from heat and add vanilla and bourbon.
4. Serve warm.

Yield: 10 people
Prep time: 20 min

Chef Kevin

134   CHOCOLATE CREPE CAKE

Ingredients

¾ cup All-purpose flour   Pinch Kosher salt
3 Eggs beaten   6 tsp Melted butter
¾ cup + 3 tsp Whole milk   2 tbsp Sugar

2 cups Heavy cream   1 ½ lbs Bittersweet chocolate

Instructions

1. Heat cream to simmer.
2. Remove from heat.
3. Add to chocolate.
4. Wait 15 seconds—then whisk to smooth.

Yield: 1 pie (8 people)
Prep time: 45 min

Chef Kevin

135   VIENNESE POTATO SALAD

Ingredients

1 ¾ lbs Waxy yellow potatoes
Boil whole.
Cool slightly, then peel.
Slice ⅛ inch rounds.

½ cup Beef broth
5 tbsp Olive oil
Pinch Kosher salt
Pinch White pepper
1 bunch Chives
1 tsp Dijon mustard

1 tsp Chopped dry or fresh
   tarragon
1 Red onion ¼ inch diced
2 tsp Sugar
3 tbsp White wine vinegar

Instructions

1. Mix dressing together.
2. Add to warm potatoes.
3. Serve warm or cold.

Yield: 10 people
Prep time: 30 min

Chef Kevin

136

SMOKY PEPPER JACK DUTCH OVEN BREAD

Ingredients

3 cups Bread flour

1 cup Whole wheat flour

1 tbsp Kosher salt

1 tbsp Smoked paprika

2 tsp Yeast

1 tsp Ground black pepper

1 ¼ cups Pepper jack cheese ¼ inch diced

1 ¾ + 2 tbsp H20, warm (110 or less)

Instructions

1. Mix above in mixer with bread hook till a ball forms.
2. Add more flour if still sticking to bowl.
3. Rise 1 hour.
4. Knead into a ball.
5. Rise ½ hour more.
6. Preheat Dutch oven ½ hour.
7. 450 cook 30 min with lid on.
8. Remove lid—8–10 more min.

Yield: 10 people

Prep time: 30 min

Chef Kevin

137   BEEF SHORT RIBS SOUS VIDE

You can sous vide beef. Keep it in the Cryovac package that you bought it in.

Short ribs
2 days (48 hours).
143 sous vide.
Season, smoke, sear, serve.
Serve with:

BBQ   Bacon butter
Chimichurri

Yield: 8 oz/per person
Prep time: 20 min

Chef Kevin

138   SOUS VIDE BRISKET

Ingredients
Brisket

Instructions
1. 137 sous vide.
2. 3 days (72 hours).
3. Remove.
4. Season, smoke, sear, serve.
5. Use beef juice to make a red wine demi glaze sauce.

Yield: 8 oz/person
Prep time: 20 min

Chef Kevin

139   CRAB BISQUE

Ingredients

Olive oil—coat pan ⅛ inch
1 cup Onion ½ to ¼ inch diced
1 cup Carrot ¼ inch diced
4 tbsp Butter—melt
6 tbsp Flour—make roux
2 Lemons juiced
10 oz H2O—dilute ½ tsp clam
    base + ½ tsp chicken base
1 tsp Shrimp bouillon powder
1 tsp Worcestershire sauce

¼ tsp Cayenne
1 tsp Shrimp bouillon
1 tbsp Kosher salt
1 tbsp Black pepper
½ tsp Old Bay
1 can Tomato paste
1 cup Heavy cream
1 can (1 lb) Crabmeat—prewarm
    to 100

Instructions

Add crab just before serving.

Yield: ½ gallon (8 people)
Prep time: 30 min

Chef Kevin

140   CHICKPEA FLOUR FLATBREAD

Ingredients

1 cup H2O	2 tsp Kosher salt
1 ¼ cups Chickpea flour	1 tsp Black pepper
1 tbsp Olive oil	1 sprig Rosemary fresh chopped

Instructions

1. Place ingredients in food processor.
2. Fry in sauté pan with about ¼ inch olive oil—fry like you would a pancake.
3. Med-high heat—golden brown on both sides.

Yield: 3–4 people
Prep time: 30 min

Chef Kevin

John 19:30
It is finished, my first cookbook. Hopefully not the last.
Thank you.
Revelations 19:16

Amen.

Chef Kevin
Ecclesiastes 3:22
So I saw that there is nothing better for a person
than to enjoy their work.
Amen.

ACKNOWLEDGMENTS

Sending thanks to the following:

The Ingram family for making this cookbook a reality. Thank you for the help and support to make this happen.

Bear Trail Lodge in King Salmon, Alaska. Nanci Lyons and family for letting us test the waters on this cookbook concept.

Jen Fry, Chef Alain Nichols, and Caleb for helping us out in Alaska.

Celia Corban for testing the blueprints for this book and letting me know that it was helpful for those getting started in the private chef world.

Patrick Lindan for taste testing a lot of my recipes and letting me use the kitchen and storage of catering equipment.

All the guests I have cooked for and who have enjoyed my recipes—use this book to make some great food at home.

1106 Design for designing this handwritten cookbook.

www.ingramcontent.com/pod-product-compliance
Lightning Source LLC
Chambersburg PA
CBHW050847150626
46549CB00012B/399